EMBROIDERY · SKILLS

APPLIQUÉ

EMBROIDERY · SKILLS

APPLIQUÉ

Pauline Brown

δελος

Published by Delos Publishers
40 Heerengracht
Cape Town

© 1989 Merehurst Limited

Edited by Diana Brinton
Designed by Bill Mason
Photography by Stewart Grant
Colour Separation by Scantrans Pte Ltd, Singapore
Printed by New Interlitho S.p.A., Milan

First edition 1989

ISBN 1-86826-054-2

CONTENTS

INTRODUCTION

Appliqué, in simplest terms, is the stitching of different fabrics to a background to create decorative pattern. One of its advantages is that it is relatively quick to do – instant effects can be produced and large areas of colour achieved. It is a versatile craft, being suitable for pictures and wallhangings, soft furnishings and clothes. In addition, the fact that it can be done either by hand or machine gives it wide appeal. For these reasons, it is a popular technique, not only with amateur needlewomen, but also with professional designers, who see its qualities as a vehicle for lavish effects in fashion, theatre design or ecclesiastical embroidery.

Appliqué has played a major part in the embroidery of Asia, where hangings, banners and animal regalia all bear patterns of fabric attached with decorative stitches. The strong tradition of European embroidery, on the other hand, has in the main been based on stitchery, but early felt and leather appliqué pieces have been found in the frozen tombs of Alma Ata in Siberia, which date from the 5th century BC. Over two millennia later, the scarcity of new fabrics stimulated inventiveness on the part of the early settlers of North America, encouraging the development of the crafts of patchwork and appliqué, so popular in the United States today.

In the long tradition of English embroidery, the use of appliqué has continued in tandem with the development of surface stitchery. During Elizabethan and Stuart times 'slips' were applied to silk or velvet grounds. The slips were so called because the designs were taken from illustrations of slips (or cuttings) in the herbals of the day. During the 17th century a similar method of three-dimensional appliqué developed. Known as stumpwork, this was highly padded and was used for decorating caskets, mirror frames and narrative pictures. The enthusiasm of the Victorian middle class for all types of fancy needlework resulted in examples of brash felt appliqué. In contrast, Jessie Newbury and Ann Macbeth, teaching at the Glasgow School of Art at the turn of the century, followed the Art

Greenhouse, *by Jane Boot, shows a contemporary approach to appliqué, using many different fabrics and other elements, such as paper and photographs, together with machine embroidery.*

Nouveau style for their designs. They used natural fabrics, such as linen and cotton, in subtle colours.

Today's embroiderers are able to build on a long and multi-national tradition, from which a wide variety of techniques have evolved – distinct styles and methods each with different characteristics and potentialities. All these methods can either be used in an orthodox fashion or they can be extended, adapted and modified. Some people prefer to conform to the precise lines of a design and to interpret the techniques in the traditional way; others may like to work in an intuitive way, using the spontaneous and random cutting of fabric and subsequent stitching to a selected background.

CHAPTER ONE

SEWING EQUIPMENT

Tools

The range of sewing tools normally found in a needlework box are almost all that are required for appliqué: that is, pins (preferably including brass lace-makers' pins, for use with fine fabrics) and needles, scissors, dressmakers' chalk, tape measure and seam ripper. In addition, a steam iron is desirable for pressing fabrics and applying iron-on interfacings, though you can use a laundry spray and an ordinary iron.

The choice of needle will depend on the task in hand – the size and type should relate to the thickness of the thread and to the weight and weave of the fabric being used. You will therefore need a selection of crewel embroidery needles; leather needles for applying leather and suede, and a circular needle for three-dimensional work. If you intend to include beads and ribbons, a beading needle and awl would be useful. Dressmakers' pins or fine brass lace pins can be used for pinning appliqué patches to a background, prior to stitching. The use of a thimble is a personal decision: it is well worth at least attempting to use one, and it will certainly be necessary when stitching tough fabrics, such as leather.

In addition to scissors kept specially for cutting paper templates and for design purposes, two further pairs are needed – a large pair for cutting out fabric and a small pair of embroidery scissors for intricate tasks and for snipping off ends of thread. For cutting decorative edges, a pair of pinking shears is a convenient extra piece of equipment.

The modern domestic sewing machine is a useful aid for appliqué. Zigzag and satin stitch provide a neat covering for raw edges, while straight stitching secures non-woven and fray-resistant fabrics satisfactorily. Built-in automatic embroidery stitches and patterns can be used to add decorative finishes to appliqué panels, garments or soft furnishings.

A good collection of fabrics and threads can often act as a starting point for an appliqué project

Threads

Ordinary sewing cotton or polyester thread is usually all that is necessary for both hand and machine appliqué. Generally, it is the practice to sew cotton with cotton, synthetic with synthetic, especially if the article will require laundering.

For additional embroidery on appliqué, there is a large number of options, including cotton embroidery threads, such as stranded and perlé cotton, coton à broder and soft embroidery thread. Silk and linen threads may enhance a piece of appliqué, and embroidery wools, which are primarily sold for canvaswork, may also be used, provided the fabric and background allow. Knitting and crochet yarns offer exciting possibilities, particularly for inclusion in wall-hangings and appliqué pictures. Thick chunky wools add texture, while fine crochet threads ensure strength for the attachment of appliqué shapes.

Fabrics

It is important to choose the right type of fabric or fabrics for a design. If the work is to be purely decorative, it will be the visual impact or the texture, in addition to the appliqué technique, that will determine your choice. If you are decorating clothes or soft furnishings, durability and laundering may be important considerations. For these reasons, it is useful to know something about fabrics and the fibres from which they are made up.

Cotton fabrics, including lawn, poplin, voile, velvet, corduroy and firmly woven cotton can all be used either for background fabrics or for appliqué patches. Most are washable, and dress-weight cotton is washable and easy to sew, making it particularly good for practice pieces, or for traditional turned-edge appliqué. Like most natural fibres, silk takes dye well and is washable. The many different types and weights range from finest Honan to chunky silk tweeds. Some silks, such as chiffon or organza, are transparent, making them suitable for shadow appliqué or decorative panels requiring translucent effects.

Wool and other animal hairs, such as angora and cashmere, besides their warmth, have a soft feel that can enhance an appliqué. Tweeds, with their unique texture and patterning, can also provide inspiration.

Manmade fibres, such as polyester, nylon, acrylic or rayon, are generally washable and often require little ironing. This makes them ideal for appliqué on everyday clothes. On the other hand, many manmade fibres have a springy quality that makes a crisp hem or turning difficult to achieve. This is generally not a problem with machine appliqué, however, where turnings are not necessary.

Non-woven fabrics, such as felt and interfacing, together with leather and suede, are suitable for many types of appliqué: they do not fray or stretch and are easy to apply, as there is no direction of weave to worry about.

Knitted fabrics are difficult to handle as backgrounds, though you can use a firm, woven backing, but their stretchy quality makes them ideal for padded appliqué and they can be manipulated to form textured areas on a decorative panel.

Batting (wadding), which is essential for padded appliqué, is generally made of silk, cotton or polyester. Polyester batting is available in several thicknesses and is practical for most purposes, as it is washable and dry-cleanable.

As well as the conventional fabrics, experiments may be made with materials such as different types of paper and plastics. In combination with machine stitching, these can provide an exciting outlet for creative ideas.

Many artists are finding that appliqué makes it possible to explore texture and colour at the same time, as in this abstract panel by Prue Dobinson.

Frames

Embroidery frames are an essential part of appliqué equipment. Most techniques can be carried out much more successfully if the fabric is mounted in a frame for stitching, as the correct tension of the stitching can be retained and the work will remain smooth and unwrinkled, with little need for additional pressing or stretching.

If the background fabric is sufficiently firm, it can be placed directly in the frame, provided you leave a wide enough margin to allow for framing. In many cases, however, it is better to baste the appliqué background to a larger piece of backing fabric (see page 16).

Hoop frames

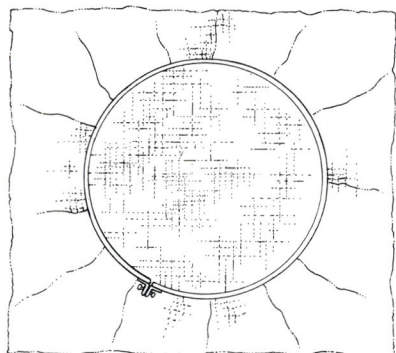

1 To dress a ring frame – in other words, put the backing or background fabric in the frame – first adjust the screw of the outer frame so that it fits loosely over the inner ring. Lay the inner ring on a flat surface and cover it with the fabric, face up.

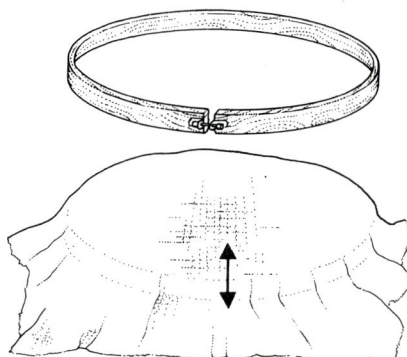

2 Press the outer ring over the fabric and the inner ring, ensuring that the warp and weft are at right angles. If not, repeat the process. (It is not advisable to pull the fabric once it has been mounted.) Tighten the screw to secure the fabric.

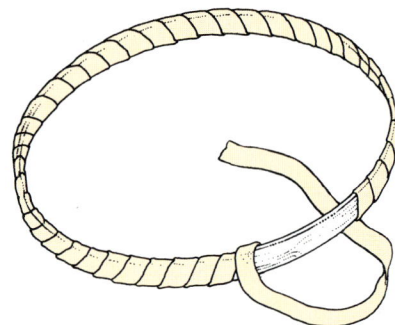

3 For free machine appliqué, and to protect delicate fabrics, the inner ring should be bound diagonally with bias seam binding along its entire length. The ring must be completely covered and the two ends of seam binding stitched firmly together.

There are three basic types of frame – the hoop, the slate and the stretcher. The choice depends on your personal preference and the size of the design. In the majority of cases the frame needs to be large enough to accommodate the whole design. Some frames are fitted with a special stand or a clamp, leaving both hands free for sewing. Alternatively, the frame can be placed on the edge of a table and weighted on one side with a heavy object, such as a book.

Hoop frames (1, 2, 3, 4)
These consist of two wooden, metal or plastic rings, the outer one being normally fitted with a screw mechanism, which can be tight-

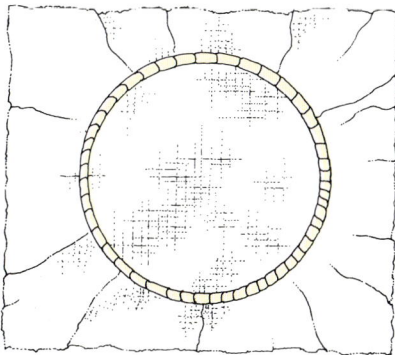

Stretcher frames

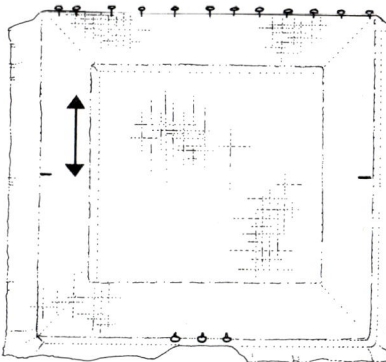

4 For machine appliqué, the fabric in the embroidery hoop must lie flat on the bed of the machine. To dress a hoop for machine work, therefore, place the fabric face down over the inner ring. Fit the outer ring and then turn the hoop over and work from this side.

5 To dress a stretcher frame, the fabric to be stretched should be cut on the straight grain and should be slightly larger than the frame. Mark the centre point at each side of the frame and make corresponding marks on the fabric. Starting at the top edge, align the centre marks and secure the fabric to the frame with a drawing pin. Continue fastening with drawing pins at 12mm (½in.) intervals, working out to the sides.
   Turn the frame and fasten the fabric to the opposite edge in the same way, stretching the fabric taut.

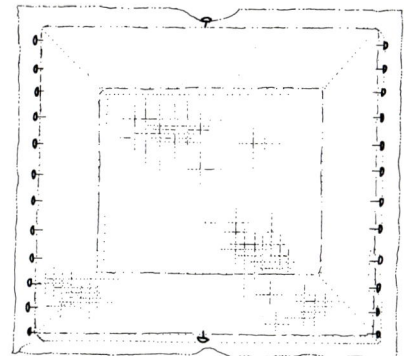

6 Secure the centre points at each side with drawing pins and continue working out towards the edges, pinning first one side and then the other. Check that the warp and weft threads are at right angles and that the fabric is stretched taut.

ened to hold the fabric securely between the two. Hoop frames are only suitable for small areas of appliqué or for isolated motifs on a larger piece of fabric. (If the hoop were re-located on to a previously worked area, it would tend to crush the stitches and damage the appliqué.) However, for free machine embroidery techniques, a hoop frame, bound with bias seam binding to protect and hold the fabric securely, is essential.

Stretcher frames (5,6)

Stretcher frames are made up of four lengths of soft wood, usually with mitred corners. They can be purchased from art shops as sets of four even lengths and interchanged to produce rectangles, as necessary, making this type of frame suitable for most hand appliqué techniques. An old picture frame of suitable dimensions would be a good substitute.

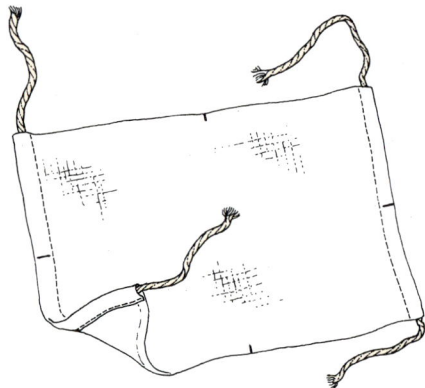

1 Mark the centre point at each side of the backing or background fabric, and press a 12mm (½in.) hem on the top and bottom edges, then a 2.5cm (1in.) hem on the side edges. Cut two lengths of string at least 50cm (20in.) longer than the sides; place these inside the side hems and machine stitch a casing over each string.

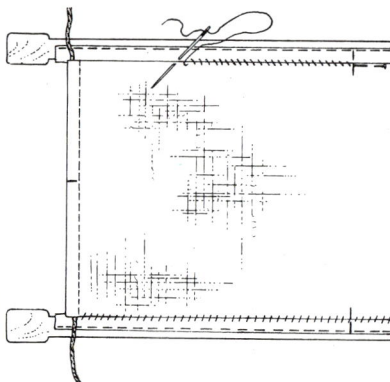

2 With wrong sides together, align the centre points on the top and bottom edges of the fabric with those on the roller tape. Pin each edge in position and then firmly overcast fabric and tape together, using linen or doubled buttonhole twist.

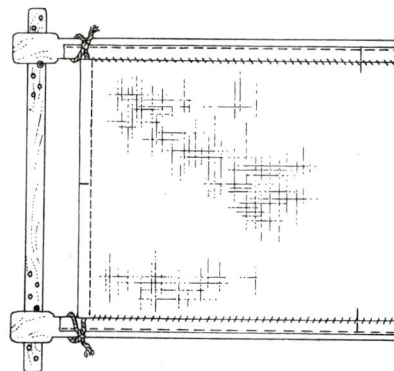

3 Insert the side battens through the rollers and secure them with the pegs, stretching the fabric fairly taut. Tie the ends of the string to the rollers.

Slate frames (1, 2, 3, 4, 5)

Slate (also known as roller or tapestry) frames comprise two rollers, each with tape attached, held apart by side battens and adjusted with pegs or split pins. The advantage of slate frames is that the tension can be adjusted very easily while the work is in progress. The width of the backing fabric (or the background, if a supporting backing is not being used) is governed by the dimensions of the tape, but the length can exceed that of the side battens, in which case the excess fabric is wound around the rollers.

Although setting your work in a slate frame may seem a time-consuming and tedious process, it is well worth the effort: the work will be held firmly, adjusted to the correct tension for your stitching; sewing will be easier, and the end result will look more professional.

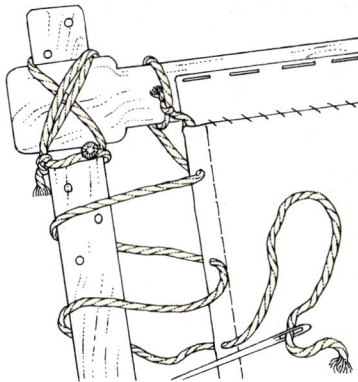

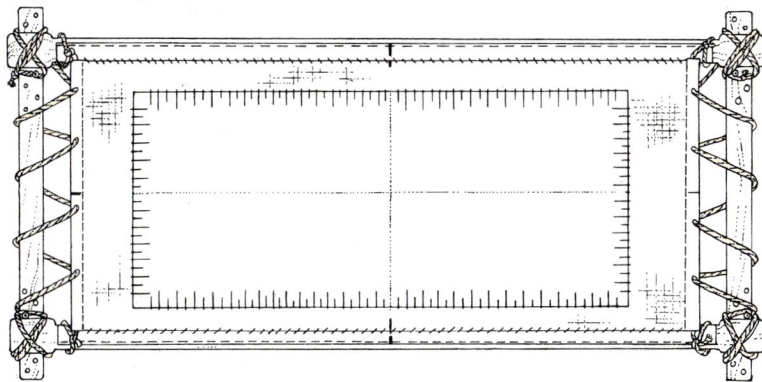

4 With a large-eyed needle, threaded with string, lace the sides of the fabric to the side battens, taking the lacing over the side and around the reinforcing strings. Pull the strings to tighten the fabric so that the sides are perpendicular to the top and bottom. Tie the string ends around the batten ends and the rollers.

5 To attach the appliqué background fabric to the stretched backing, slightly loosen the tension of the backing fabric and place the background fabric centrally on this, pinning at intervals. Overcast the raw edges with alternate long and short stitches to distribute the tension. Re-stretch, so that the fabric is taut.

CHAPTER TWO

BASIC APPLIQUÉ TECHNIQUES

Preparation for appliqué

Careful preparatory work will help to ensure the success of a piece of appliqué. Each technique has its own particular characteristics, making it necessary to use the appropriate method of cutting out and positioning the pieces. In some cases, the whole design is transferred to a backing fabric, or it can be drawn on the background material, with the corresponding appliqué patches stitched in place. For other methods, the cut out shapes may be assembled by eye, either covering a supporting backing or set against a background.

Backing fabrics

Although it is not essential for every type of appliqué, some methods, such as stained glass appliqué, folded star and clamshell patchwork, require a backing fabric. This is not the same as a background fabric, because unlike the latter, which is visible, a backing fabric acts as a support, but does not show on the finished work, which is completely covered by the appliqué. Light-weight and stretch background fabrics also need a backing to add firmness and strength, while wallhangings and panels benefit from the extra weight that this treatment gives. The backing fabric, which should be pre-washed, should as far as possible correspond in weight to the background – cotton lawn is suitable for most fine fabrics, calico for other types. The background fabric, which should be at least 10cm (4in.) larger than the finished size of the embroidery, to allow for seams, hems or mounting, is tacked on top of the framed backing fabric, with the straight grain of both aligned.

Positioning the design (1, 2)

Positioning the design on the background fabric is usually a simple matter, and may be done by eye, but in some cases, such as a centrally placed design, it may be necessary to be more precise.

1 To position a design, first find the centre of the design by folding it into quarters and marking two pencil lines along the folds, crossing at the centre. To check that you have the exact centre, either draw a diagonal or simply lay a ruler from corner to corner – the diagonal should run across the meeting point of the horizontal and vertical lines.

2 | The centre of the fabric can be found by folding this in a similar way and marking the corresponding lines with two rows of tacking stitches. When you transfer the design, the two sets of markings can be aligned.

The correct order of assembly, starting with the background pieces and gradually progressing towards the foreground, can clearly be seen in Spanish village, *by Diane Langleben, which uses the turned-edge method of appliqué.*

Transferring the design (1, 2)

The first stage of most appliqué techniques is to make a full-scale drawing of the design. This may be done on tracing paper and should show the outlines only. When you have transferred the design to the paper, enlarging or reducing it as necessary (see page 125), run over the lines with a black felt-tip pen. Number each separate appliqué shape on the design in order of assembly (see below). This paper design is used to make templates, to transfer the design to the background fabric, and to act as a reference during sewing.

The simplest method of transferring the design to the background fabric is by direct tracing. This is suitable if the background fabric or backing is light in colour and fairly thin. If the outlines do not show through clearly you may be able to see them if you tape the design and then the fabric to a window. Alternatively, try laying them on a glass-topped table, with a lamp underneath. If the fabric is too thick or too dark for this method, use dressmakers' carbon paper. This is used in a similar way to office carbon, which is not suitable, as it is too smudgy and will leave indelible marks. Dressmakers' carbon can be purchased from fabric stores and is available in several colours, so choose the one that is closest in tone to the background fabric. As well as transferring the design to the background fabric, dressmakers' carbon can also be used to mark the outlines of applied shapes and motifs.

Preparing paper templates (3)

Most appliqué consists of precise shapes that correspond to areas of the original drawing, so unless you are using dressmakers' carbon paper, paper patterns or templates must be cut from a tracing. If the design is complex, the pieces can each be marked with a number, indicating the order of application and relating to the numbers on the original design.

Transferring the design

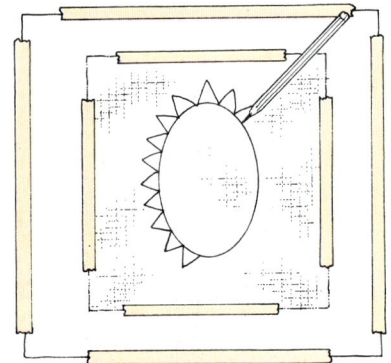

1 To trace directly onto a fabric, tape the design to a flat surface and place the background fabric over it, right side up. Hold it in place with masking tape. Using a fabric marker, a chalk pencil or a hard pencil, trace around the design outlines. If you cannot see the design through the fabric, either use a light box or tape both the design and the fabric to a window pane (during daylight hours) and trace over the lines.

Preparing paper templates

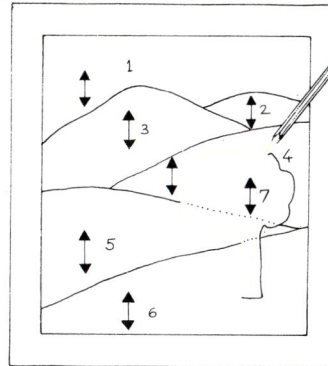

Order of assembly

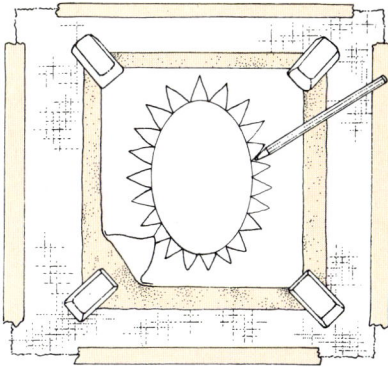

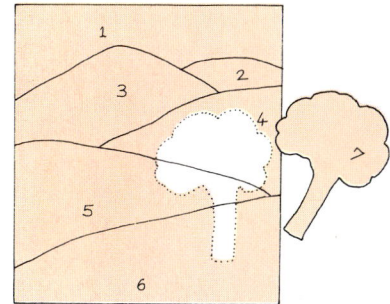

2 To use dressmakers' carbon, tape the fabric to a flat surface and position the design on top, holding it in place with weights or tape. Slip the dressmakers' carbon paper, coloured (inked) side down between the two. Use an empty ballpoint pen, a blunt-ended knitting needle or a similar blunt tool to trace firmly over the lines of the design.

3 To prepare templates, make a tracing of the design and number each shape, copying the design numbers and indicating the vertical alignment of each piece with an arrow. This will enable you to make sure that you cut out each shape with the grainlines running in the same direction as the background fabric. Cut out each paper pattern and use it according to the appliqué method that you have chosen.

4 Sections of a design should be applied in a logical order, overlapping as necessary. For example, when assembling a landscape, it is best to start with the pieces in the background and gradually superimpose the separate sections until the foreground is complete. Design sections that will ultimately be overlapped by other pieces may, if this is simpler, be cut out as whole pieces rather than as intricate shapes.

Assembling appliqué (4)

If the design has been transferred to the background by direct tracing or dressmakers' carbon paper, the cut-out shapes are positioned over the marked outlines. In some cases, motifs may be assembled by eye, with the pieces moved around until a satisfactory arrangement is achieved. This is particularly appropriate for Persian appliqué, the patchwork appliqué methods and for some designs in which the basic turned-edge, raw-edge and padded techniques are used. Alternatively, if a tracing is taken of the design, this can be placed over the fabric and the appliqué pieces can then be slipped between the two and moved around until they coincide with the traced shapes.

Backing pieces

Traditionally, appliqué pieces were not backed before being applied to the background, and it is by no means necessary always to back pieces. Modern iron-on interfacing and fusible web can, however, be very useful.

Iron-on interfacings (1, 2, 3)

Iron-on interfacing is available in a wide range of thicknesses and qualities. Some interfacings are designed to support jersey and other stretch fabrics and are best used for that purpose, whereas thick craft interfacing could as well be used for a fine cotton as for a heavy wool, provided a stiff, bold piece of appliqué is required. For blind appliqué, iron-on interfacing gives a firm edge over which to fold the allowance. Flimsy fabrics can be given extra 'body', and interfacing also helps to disguise the turned edge of such fabrics from showing through. Fabrics that fray and those that are slippery or difficult to handle can also benefit.

In some cases, interfacing a fabric patch will make it unnecessary to match the straight grain with that of the background. A fabric can therefore be applied at another angle if the design dictates; for example, because a diagonal weave or pattern provides a crucial element. For articles that need to drape, however, the grain of the appliqué must correspond to that of the background.

For machine appliqué, iron the interfacing to the fabric and cut out the motif, without a turning, then apply it with machine zigzag. This method is not suitable for very frayable fabrics.

Fusible web (4, 5, 6)

This paper-backed, double-sided bonding is particularly suitable for Persian and stained glass appliqué, and for the machine appliqué of frayable fabrics. It gives an immaculate result and can bond fabrics together to create free-standing cut-outs. Experiment before embarking on a project – the technique may not be satisfactory if you are applying a fine fabric to a heavily textured background, as the imprint of the latter will be visible. The effect of transparent fabrics will be somewhat altered by the adhesive that shows through.

Iron-on interfacings

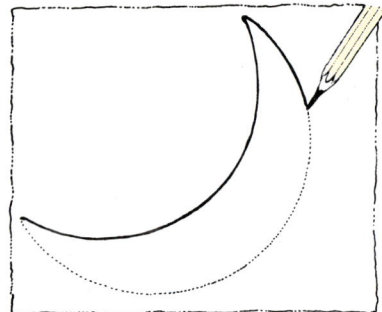

1 Place the interfacing, shiny (adhesive) side up, over the design and trace, using a hard pencil or a fabric marker. If you are using a template, place this right side up on the shiny side of the interfacing and trace around the shape. Mark the grainline and pattern number on the non-adhesive side.

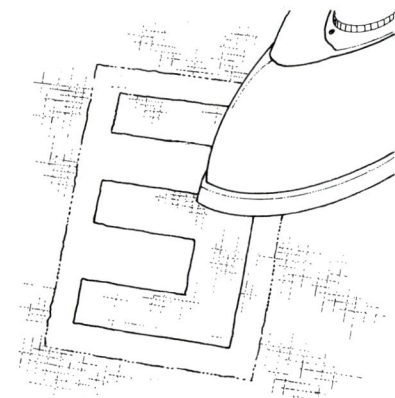

5 Cut out the fusible web motif or pattern, allowing a margin all round, and place this rough (adhesive) side down on the wrong side of the fabric, matching grainlines if necessary, and iron.

Using fusible web

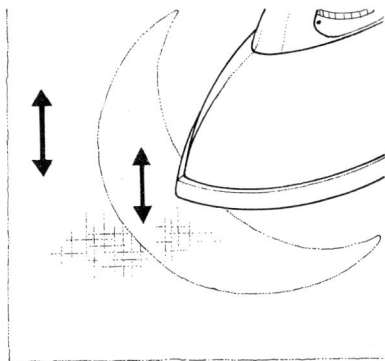

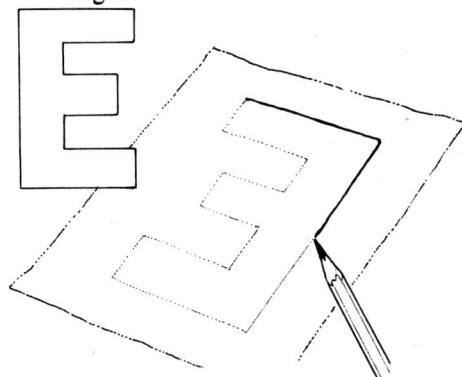

Cut out the shape and place it, shiny side down, on the wrong side of the fabric, aligning the grain if necessary. Carefully press with a steam iron, set to the appropriate heat setting.

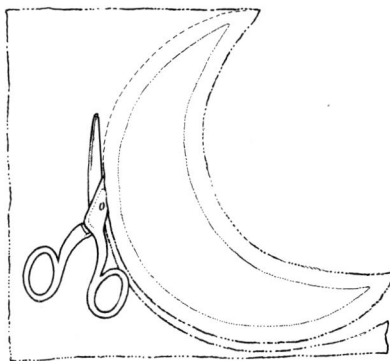

Cut out around the perimeter of the shape, leaving a seam allowance of between 6mm and 12mm (¼in. and ½in.), depending on the size and shape of the piece and the type of fabric. The seam allowance can then be folded over the edge of the interfacing.

4 To use fusible web, place it, smooth (non-adhesive) side up, over the reverse side of the design tracing. If you are using a template, place this with the wrong side up over the fusible web, which should be smooth side up. Trace over the outline, to make a mirror (reverse) image of the pattern piece. Mark the grainline and pattern number on the smooth side.

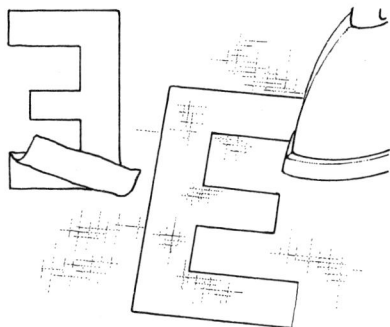

6 When cool, cut out the shape through the backing paper and fabric, cutting along the design outline. Peel off the backing and position the shape on the background fabric and iron firmly.

Basic hand appliqué

Non-woven fabrics, such as felt, leather, suede and interfacings have many practical advantages for use in appliqué, as they do not fray, stretch or distort; there is no need to turn under the edges of motifs, and consideration need not be given to aligning the straight grain. Although they can, of course, be attached with fusible web, it is also not usually necessary to interline them, as they are substantial enough in themselves.

Non-woven fabrics, together with net, can all be cut out and applied directly with stab stitch or slip stitch. For these reasons they are often chosen by beginners as the easiest option, but it is advisable that they are selected for their aesthetic qualities rather than their ease of application. The mat surface of brightly coloured felt would, for instance, enhance a simple nursery panel, but could bring an unwanted naivety to a more sophisticated piece.

Marking and cutting out (1, 2)

There are several ways of marking and cutting out motifs – much depends on your personal preference, but some methods are more suitable for certain materials than others. For example, it is difficult to make marks on felt, so this is best cut out by pinning a paper pattern to it, whereas suede and leather shapes should be marked on the reverse side with a fabric marker, as it is not possible to use pins. Remember, when marking on the reverse side, to position the template right side down, or the cut shape will be a mirror image, not an exact copy.

Applying shapes without seam allowances (3, 4)

Shapes cut from non-frayable fabrics can be attached without turnings, but it is also possible to stitch frayable fabrics in position without turning the edges under. It is, however, important to take account of their frayable qualities and to handle the pieces as gently as possible. Fabrics that are difficult to handle may be backed with iron-on interfacing and cut out, omitting seam allowances. Alternatively, fusible web, which produces a flatter effect than interfacing, can be used to adhere the shape and prevent fraying.

1 If the fabric can be marked directly, place the paper or cardboard template, right side down, on the back of the fabric and draw around it. Cut out the shape along the marked line.

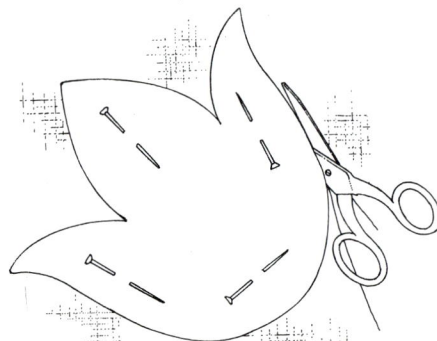

2 If the fabric cannot easily be marked, pin the paper template, right side down, on the back of the fabric. Cut around the shape, without seam allowances.

Applying shapes

3 Mark the design on the background fabric and either frame it or baste it in position on the framed backing fabric, if you are using one (see page 20). Pin the cut-out shape in place, fitting it to the design marked on the background. Baste it in place with diagonal stitches, smoothing out any folds or wrinkles as you proceed. Secure the appliqué with your chosen stitch (see page 26), and remove basting stitches.

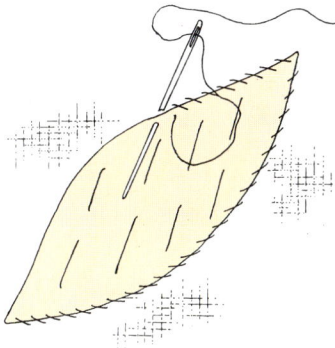

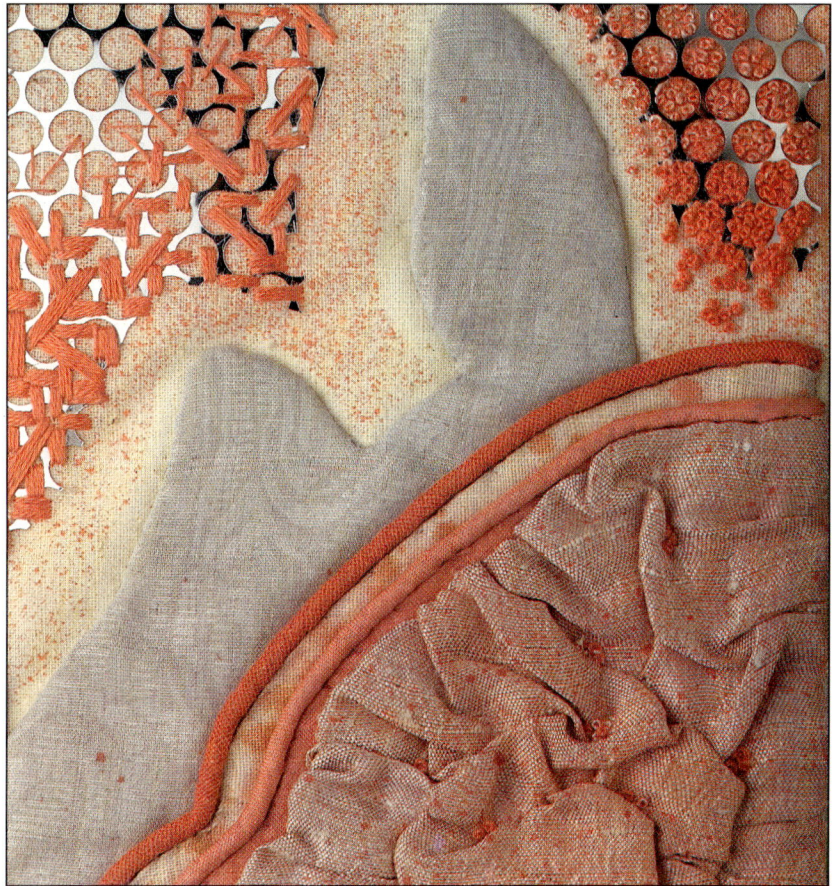

4 To attach a frayable fabric without seam allowances, cut out the shape and baste it in position on the framed background. (If fusible web or interfacing is to be used, see page 20.) Overcast the edges with a thread that matches the colour of the appliqué shape. Conceal the overcasting with a decorative stitch, and remove basting stitches.

This sample by Prue Dobinson shows variations on the turned-edge method, using a sprayed background, a manipulated fabric section, piping and sequin waste.

Turned-edge (blind) appliqué

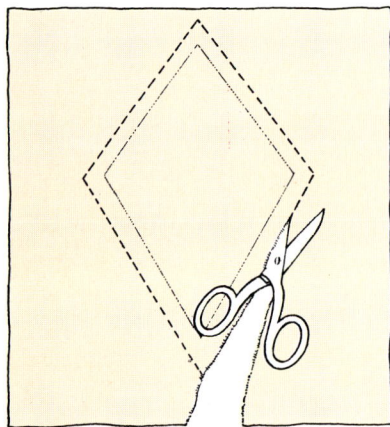

Turned-edge appliqué (1, 2, 3) is suitable for fabrics that fray and for those fine enough to allow a hem to be turned under neatly. It is used where a blind edge, without decorative stitching, is required. It is also used for padded appliqué, in which the motif is stitched over felt or batting. Iron-on interfacing, though not essential, can be used as a backing, producing an edge over which the hem may be turned.

Curves, points and corners (4, 5, 6)

To achieve a neat professional finish, in which every detail and subtlety of shape is retained, careful manipulation of the seam

Turned-edge appliqué

1 Follow the instructions for marking and cutting out non-woven fabrics, but add a seam allowance all around of between 6mm and 12mm (¼in. and ½in.), depending on the size, shape and fabric of the piece.

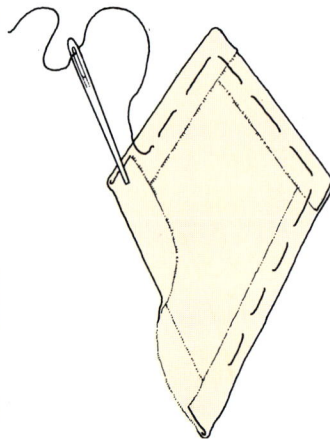

2 If you choose, interline the shapes with iron-on interfacing, cut to the size of the finished motif. If not, machine a row of stay-stitching along the marked stitching line. Fold the seam allowance to the wrong side, using the edge of the interfacing or the stay-stitching as a guide. Snip, notch or trim allowances as necessary, and baste them in place, using a fine needle and thread.

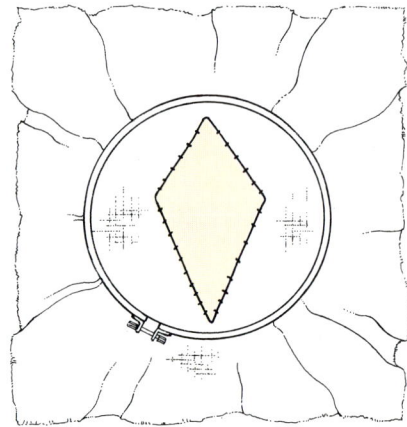

3 Mark the design on the background fabric and frame it (and backing, if desired). Pin the prepared shape in place and baste with diagonal stitches, smoothing away any folds as you proceed. Secure the appliqué with your chosen stitch and remove basting stitches.

allowances is essential. Straight edges present few problems, but curves, points and corners must be handled as shown.

Rouleaux strips

For narrow strips of appliqué, for example flower stems, rouleaux strips may be used. To make these, simply cut a bias strip to double the required width, plus a 6mm (¼in.) seam allowance on either side. Fold the strip in half lengthwise, with right sides together, and stitch, with back stitch or machine stitching. Attach a strong thread to one end of the strip and push the needle, eye forward, through the fold, turning the strip right side out. The strip can then be slipstitched in place, with stitches running along each edge.

Curves, points and corners

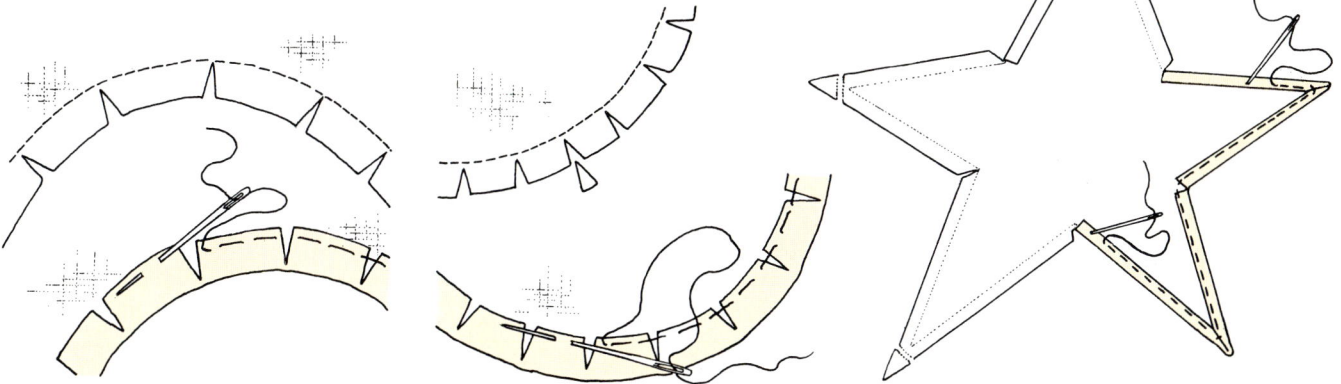

4 At concave (inward) curves, snip the excess almost up to the stay-stitching (or to within 3mm/⅛in. of the interfacing), making cuts at regular intervals. Using a fine needle and thread, fold the allowance over and baste it in place with small stitches.

5 At convex (outward) curves, remove small notches of fabric from the seam allowance at regular intervals, in order to reduce the excess bulk that will otherwise show when the fabric is folded. Again, snip to within 3mm (⅛in.) of the stay-stitching or interfacing.

6 On outer corners and at acute angles, trim the point to reduce bulk. Fold the corner down first, then the two adjacent sides. Baste the seam allowance in place as for curves. On inner corners, slit the fabric up to the stay-stitching or interfacing, in order to turn back the sides.

Appliqué stitches

A small repertoire of basic stitches for appliqué have traditionally been used to secure the stitches firmly but unobtrusively to the background. Each produces a slightly different effect, and a stitch should be chosen for its suitability in relation to the design and the fabrics being used. Ordinary cotton thread is the usual thread, but pure silk or polyester threads may also be used in combination with fabrics of those fibres.

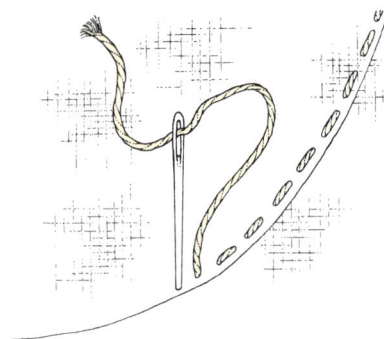

1 Stab stitch is worked to form a dotted line, with tiny stitches evenly spaced in a line parallel with the edge of the applied shape. It differs from running stitch in that the needle pierces the fabric vertically instead of diagonally. It is suitable for non-fray fabrics and also for attaching free-standing motifs, such as lace flowers or fabric leaves.

Couching in soft embroidery cotton is used to define the edge of the stones in this sample by Doreen Brewster.

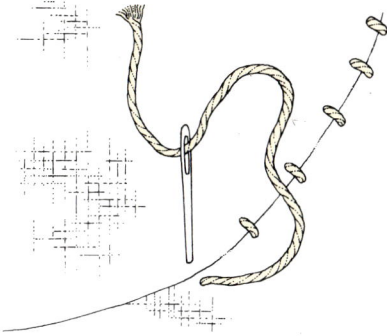

2 Slip stitch is mostly used for turned-edge (blind) appliqué and should be worked so as to be as unobtrusive as possible. The needle is brought up through the background fabric, close to the edge of the motif, and a tiny straight stitch is worked into the turned edge. This is repeated at regular intervals of about 6mm (¼in.).

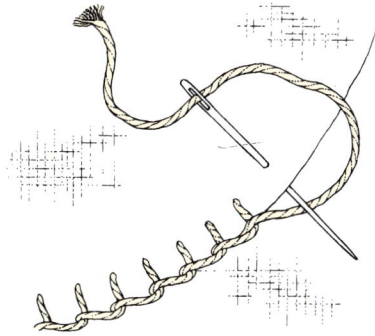

3 Buttonhole stitch featured a great deal in appliqué work of the past. It should, however, be used with discretion as, although it serves the purpose of securing the fabric in place, it can look primitive and child-like. It should therefore be worked very neatly, with tiny stitches, to create a firm decorative edge that need not impose itself too much on the design.

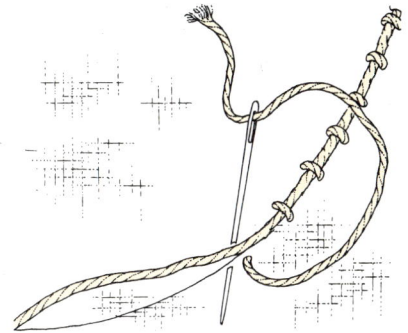

4 Couching involves the use of two threads – one laid along the edge of the applied motif and another, finer, one fastening it down. When working this stitch, it is essential to mount the fabric in a frame in order to retain the correct tension. This is a useful method, as the laid threads can be discreet if toning colours are used; alternatively, a more defined outline can be created with decorative yarns which would otherwise be too thick and would not pull through the fabric.

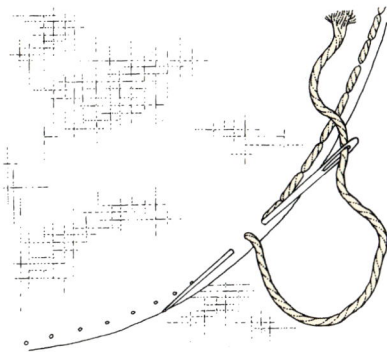

5 Back stitch produces a continuous line of stitches of even length, similar to machine stitches. It is particularly satisfactory for attaching leather or suede, in which case you should use a leather needle and strong thread. To facilitate stitching thick leather or hide, a preparatory line of holes can be made by using the sewing machine without thread.

Basic machine appliqué

The advantage of machine appliqué lies not only in its speed, but also in the firmness and strength of the stitching. This makes it an ideal medium for decorating hardwearing articles, such as children's clothes and everyday household items, including table linen and bedlinen that need to stand up to frequent laundering. The appearance of machine-applied motifs differs from those attached by hand in that they acquire a crispness of definition and, if satin stitch is used, a boldly accentuated outline.

Before embarking on machine appliqué, it is essential to become fully conversant with the working of your machine and to know how to alter the stitch length and width for zigzag and satin stitch. Some sewing machines have a special appliqué foot in transparent plastic: this is particularly useful, as it enables the operator to see exactly where the needle will pierce the edge of the fabric.

Machine zigzag creates a textured pattern of grasses while simultaneously securing pieces of fabric in this panel by Sheila Cahn.

Applying motifs (1, 2, 3)

Two of the most commonly used methods of applying motifs are with fusible web (1), which will help to adhere intricate raw-edged motifs to a background, thereby creating an immaculate finish, and the stitch-and-cut method (2, 3). This is suitable for designs that incorporate bold shapes, and it is especially useful for fine fabrics, including any that may fray.

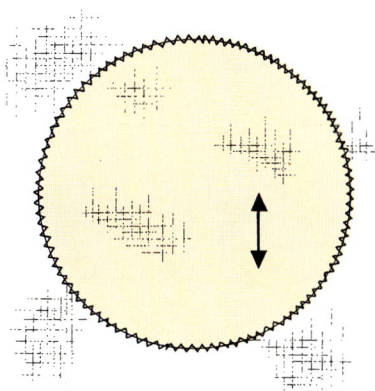

1 If you are using the fusible web method, bond the motif in place in the normal way, matching the grain with that of the background fabric. Work a line of zigzag stitching to cover the edge, adjusting your machine to a suitable stitch width and length for each motif.

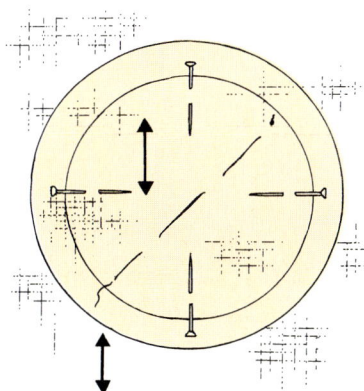

2 For the stitch-and-cut method, first transfer the outline of the appliqué shape to the right side of the fabric and cut it out, leaving a 2cm (¾in.) margin all round. Pin the shape to the background fabric, matching grains and with the pins placed at right angles to the marked outline. If necessary, secure with a few diagonal basting stitches.

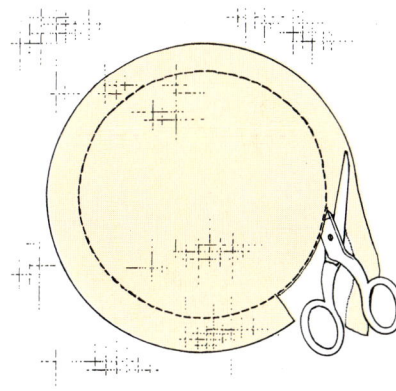

3 Machine with straight stitch on the marked line, working in a clockwise direction. Using small, pointed, embroidery scissors, trim away any excess fabric close to the stitching. If the appliqué is likely to be subjected to hard wear or frequent washing, the single line of machine stitches should be covered with a row of zigzag or close satin stitch, after the excess fabric has been trimmed.

Stitching

It is not usually necessary to hem the edges of appliqué shapes that are to be machined, unless you are intending to use straight stitching in conjunction with fabrics that may fray. If this is the case, follow the instructions already given for the turned-edge method, replacing the final hand stitching with machine sewing.

Most machine appliqué employs zigzag or satin stitch on raw-edged motifs, this being the method with most strength, although free machining and decorative automatic stitches may also be used. For most purposes, ordinary cotton or polyester thread is suitable, but machine embroidery thread gives a fine, glossy effect that may be appropriate for some designs.

Ordinary straight stitching, in conjunction with either the turned-edge or stitch-and-cut methods, is often used for attaching appliqué shapes to a background. Provided you are fully acquainted with your machine, you will have few problems. It is best to use a short stitch rather than a long one, particularly for attaching intricately shaped motifs.

Zigzag stitching provides a neat but strong method of applying bolder shapes. The width and length of the zigzag can be adjusted in order to create different decorative effects, which can be selected according to the artistic and practical requirements of the design.

Zigzag shaping (1, 2, 3, 4)

Attaching shapes with zigzag or satin stitch is not difficult, but you may need to practise turning at corners, points and tight curves if you are to achieve an immaculate finish. The shapes should either be bonded or pinned and basted in place, and the machine stitching carried out slowly and carefully.

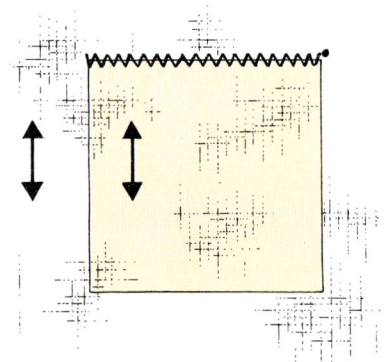

1 For outside corners, work zigzag or satin stitch to the corner, stopping the machine with the needle to the right. With the needle still in the fabric, pivot the work and continue stitching along the next side.

In this sample by Doreen Brewster, similar types of lurex and net fabric have been layered over paper and stitched, after which some have been cut away to reveal underlying layers. The stitching shows the hard-edged effect of satin stitching on a paper background.

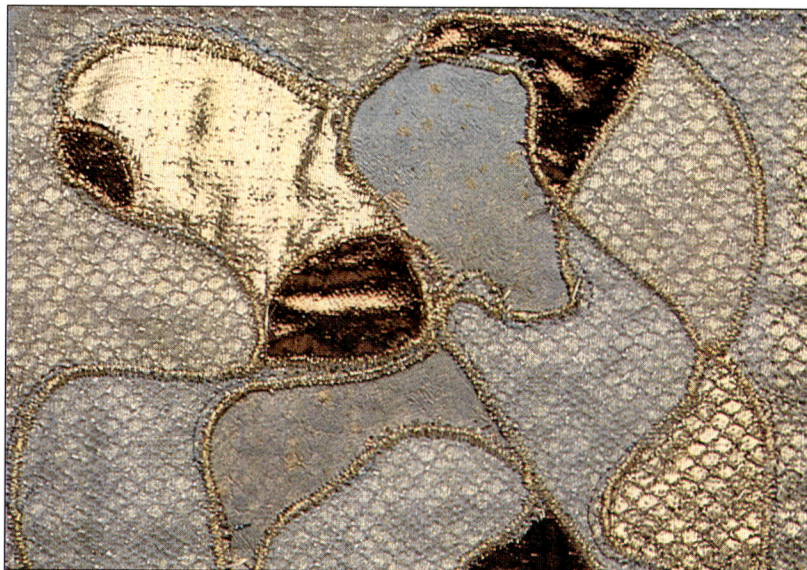

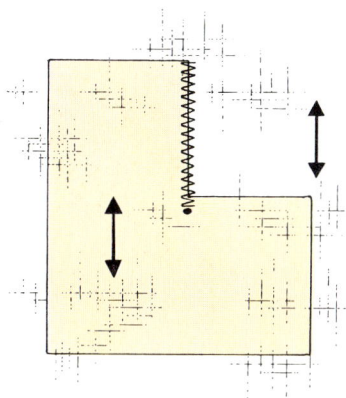

2 Inside corners are worked as for outside corners, but stop the machine with the needle to the left. Pivot as for outside corners and continue stitching.

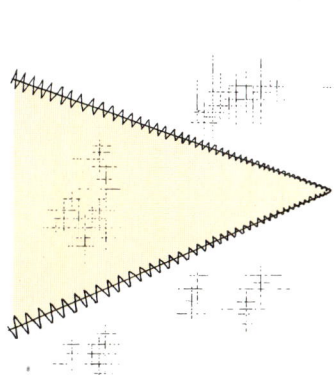

3 For acute points and inward corners, the zigzag may be tapered by gradually narrowing the stitch width towards the corner. With the needle still in the fabric, pivot the work and stitch down the other side, gradually increasing the stitch width.

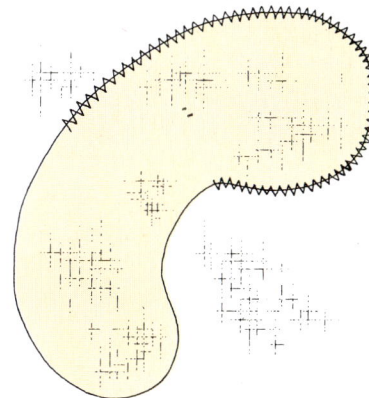

4 Shallow curves present no problem and can be stitched as for straight edges. When stitching a zigzag around a tight curve, pivot the work every few stitches, stopping the machine with the needle on the outside of the curve and pivoting the fabric accordingly.

31

CHAPTER THREE

APPLIQUÉ VARIATIONS

Padded appliqué

In recent years, three-dimensional items have featured prominently in the work of professional textile artists. These include appliqué panels and items such as cushions with free-standing motifs cascading from the surface, as well as completely three-dimensional objects. This type of embroidery is based on padded appliqué techniques that can be adapted or modified to suit the subject. This will add another dimension to the work, either in the form of softly textured areas of focal interest, sculptured motifs of high relief or three-dimensional shapes that project from the background fabric. The choice of padding depends not only on the raised effect required, but also on the type of fabric used and whether the item to be made is to be washed or dry-cleaned. Synthetic batting, available in several thicknesses, gives a soft squashy effect, while felt tends to be firmer, and padding with cardboard or craft interlining produces a stiff hard-edged result. All padded appliqué should be worked in a frame.

Padding with felt (1, 2)

Felt has traditionally been used extensively in ecclesiastical embroidery for padding leather and metal threadwork. It is also a suitable padding for raised areas on pictures and wallhangings, where a firm, slightly domed effect is required. It is normally used in combination with the turned-edge method of appliqué.

Padding with batting (3)

Synthetic batting (polyester wadding), which comes in several weights, is versatile, as it can be laundered, which makes it suitable for soft furnishings, such as cushions and quilts, as well as for decoration on garments. Its applications for wallhangings and appliqué panels include soft sculptural effects of high or low relief. Silk or cotton batting may also be used, but are less readily available.

Padding with batting

1 Using the paper pattern, mark and cut out a piece of felt the same size and shape as the appliqué motif; then cut several further shapes, each slightly smaller than the previous one (usually, three or four are needed).

2 Starting with the smallest, pin and stitch it to the centre of the area to be padded, using a stab stitch, worked at right angles to the edge of the felt. Repeat with the next size, stitching it on top of the first, and continue until each piece is attached. Sew the prepared appliqué shape on top, using the turned-edge method.

For an asymmetrical effect, the padding can be varied in depth, with some areas raised higher than others.

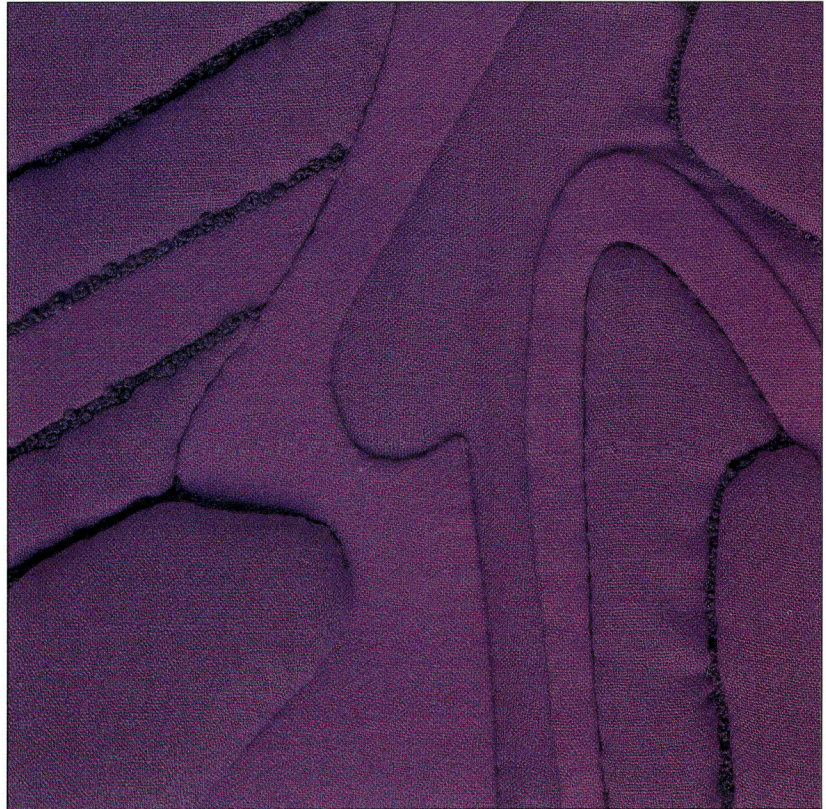

This sample by Margaret Barclay uses padded appliqué over felt, attached with the turned-edge method, for the heavily-raised areas. Card has been used as the padding for the flatter parts of the design.

3 **To use batting, prepare the appliqué shape and cut a piece of batting the same size and of the required thickness. Stitch the batting to the background fabric, using loosely tensioned straight stitches, placed at right angles to the edge. Stitch the prepared appliqué shape on top, using the turned-edge method.**

Padding with cardboard or stiff interfacing

Card is a suitable material for padding areas of appliqué pictures and panels that do not require cleaning. For garments and soft furnishings, stiff craft or pelmet interfacing is an alternative that produces a similar effect and can be drycleaned. The advantage of using this type of padding is the hard-edged effect that it creates, giving sharp definition to designs that include architectural shapes or precise geometric forms. For a hard-edged, but softer, padded effect, batting or felt can be inserted between the fabric and the cardboard. The thickness of the card is dependent upon the weight of the fabric to be applied and the size of the motif. For small and delicate motifs, light cardboard may be used; mat (mounting) board would be a satisfactory choice for a more substantial shape.

Cut a piece of cardboard or stiff craft interfacing to the size and shape of the finished appliqué motif. Cut out the fabric, making it between 6mm and 12mm (¼in. and ½in.) larger all around. Centre the cardboard on the wrong side of the fabric and apply fabric glue sparingly around the edge. Fold the fabric edges over to adhere. Curves, points and corners should be snipped, notched or trimmed as for the turned-edge method. Apply the fabric-covered cardboard to the background fabric by working slip stitches around the edge.

Left *In* Salad plate, *by Doris Lopian, padded appliqué is used to produce life-like salad vegetables. The plate and tomatoes are padded with card.*

Right *To create the comic postcard effect of* Cor! What a cheek!, *Margaret Barclay has used card, felt and wadding to pad the appliqué pieces.*

Free-standing motifs

Free-standing motifs, projecting from the surface, can add – quite literally – another dimension to an appliqué design. The shapes may be made with fusible web (1), or stuffed, with raw edges (2) or with turned edges (3,4): the choice depends on the desired end

Fusible webb

Raw edges

1 To make a free-standing motif with fusible web, first adhere two fabrics to each other, with wrong sides together. Mark the design on one side and cut the shape out. The edges will not fray, so they may be left untreated. Details can be embroidered with decorative stitches and the motif can be stiffened, if desired, by spraying it with roller blind stiffener or a weak solution of fabric adhesive. If you want to mould the piece into a particular form – to create, for example, a curled leaf, you can insert fine florists' wire between the layers before bonding, to make the piece more malleable.

2 To make a padded motif with a raw edge, first mark the design on the top fabric. Place the top fabric over the bottom fabric, with wrong sides together, and insert a layer of batting between them. (The layer of batting may, of course, be omitted if it is not needed, or felt may be substituted.) Baste the pieces together, then machine stitch along the outline.

Cut out the motif, close to the stitching. Work satin stitch or machine zigzag over the edge, or cover the cut edge with buttonhole stitch.

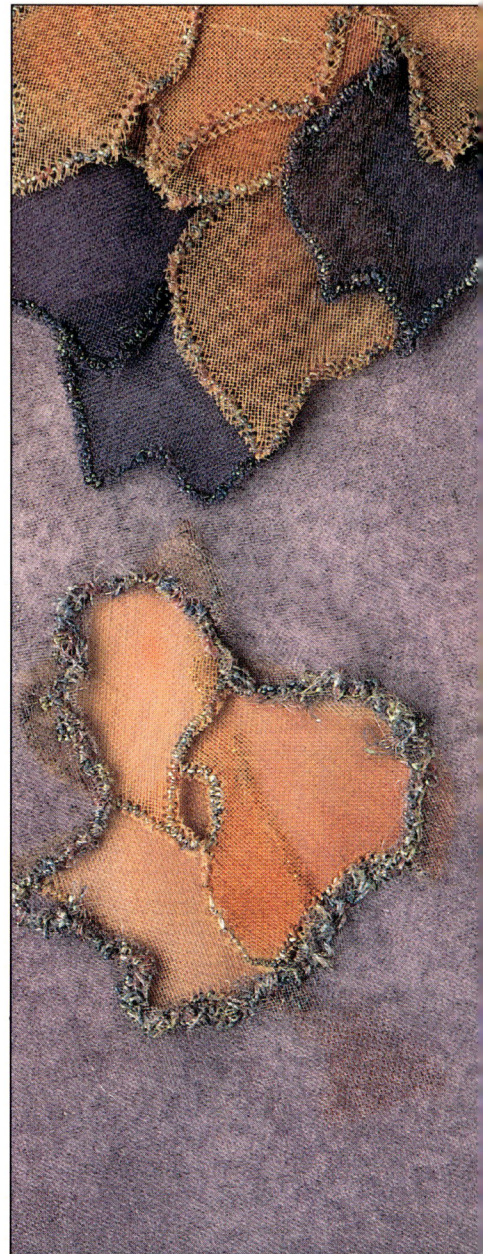

effect. This type of motif is normally attached to the background fabric only at one or two points. The bonding method is most suitable for very intricate shapes (florists' wire is often included inside the shape, which can then be manipulated), while padding – either with polyester or with felt – can add to the three-dimensional appearance.

Turned edges

3 | Mark the design on the wrong side of the top fabric. Place the top and bottom fabrics right sides together, with the batting underneath them. Baste them together, then straightstitch by machine along the outline, leaving an opening through which to turn the work.

Remove basting stitches and cut out the motif. Remember to allow for the turning, but trim excess fabric as necessary. Trim the batting close to the stitching line.

In this panel by Judy Hope, free-standing organza leaves have been edged with machine stitching, for a delicate effect.

4 | Turn the motif to the right side, turning through the opening. Press the seam lightly, and slipstitch the opening. The edge may be finished with an additional row of machine stitching or a decorative edge, sewn by hand.

Persian appliqué

Persian appliqué, also known as appliqué perse, broderie perse and cretonne appliqué, probably came from Persia as an inexpensive imitation of embroidery. It became popular in the middle of the 19th century, when birds, flowers and animals, cut from printed cretonnes, were reassembled into scrapbook effects on plain black backgrounds. The edges of the motifs were usually left raw and were stitched firmly and details of the design emphasized with embroidery in coloured silks. Popular nowadays in the United States, it is most frequently used as decoration on quilts.

It is a bold, quick and simple method, suitable for the inexperienced designer, as cut out pieces of printed fabrics may be moved around until a satisfactory effect is achieved. Fabrics that are

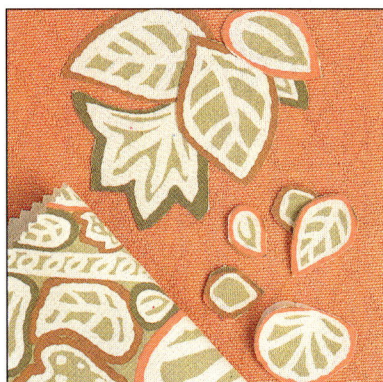

1 Carefully cut out printed motifs with small sharp scissors: if you are using fusible or iron-on interfacing, this must be applied before you cut out the motifs.

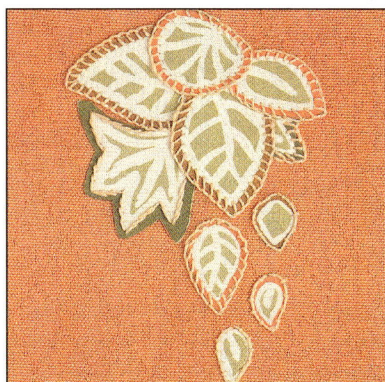

2 Arrange the motifs in such a way that the spaces between them are harmonious in shape and these areas are in proportion to the whole. Either bond or pin and tack the motifs to the ground fabric (which should preferably be mounted on a frame). Secure the edges with neat decorative stitches or use a machine stitch appropriate to the scale of the piece.

non-fray or fray-resistant are most suitable. Coordinating plain and printed fabrics can be used to advantage to decorate table linen with appliqué motifs, arranged as borders or random patterns, while smaller designs can look charming on children's T-shirts or dresses.

As the edges of the motifs are not turned under, it is a help to use a fusible web or a backing of iron-on interfacing. This can be ironed directly to the back of the printed fabric, before the shapes are cut out. Persian appliqué has traditionally been sewn by hand, using a decorative stitch, such as buttonhole stitch, to secure the appliqué in place, but motifs can be attached by machining with decorative or zigzag stitches.

In an unusual development of Persian appliqué, Elspeth Kemp has taken motifs taken from a crewel-work embroidery and set them against a contrasting background.

Reverse appliqué

The Cuña Indians of the San Blas islands off the coast of Panama are famous for this technique, which they use to create lively designs of brightly-coloured cotton, depicting legends and scenes of daily life. These *molas* are nowadays much sought after, though the modern versions do not have the same quality as those of the past. A similar technique is used by the hill tribes in Thailand, but there the work has a much more delicate and refined character.

To stitch reverse appliqué in the traditional manner requires a certain dexterity, but once mastered, the technique produces an effect that cannot be achieved in any other way. The basic method is for several pieces of fabric to be laid one on top of the other and for the layers gradually to be cut away to reveal those beneath. Fabrics should be fine and non-slip: cotton lawn is ideal. Plain contrasting colours produce the most satisfactory effects, though small prints can be used with discretion, provided the tonal value and the scale permits. Dark colours should be placed on top of light, so that the turnings do not show through, and laundering qualities should be considered if you are making garments or soft furnishings.

If you are new to this technique, choose a design that is bold and simple, making sure that the enclosed motifs have straight or shallow curved edges. It is best to avoid narrow shapes and acute angles.

Machine method

As with the hand method, choose a bold design that can easily be manoeuvred on the sewing machine. Non-fray fabrics may be stitched with straight stitch, but a close zigzag or satin stitch would be more appropriate for other types of material. The stitch width should be adjusted to relate to the scale of the areas to be cut away.

The layers of fabric are prepared in the same way as for the hand method, with two rows of additional basting both ways across the centre of the design to hold the fabrics firm. Stitch around the shape to be removed, then cut away the top layer, close to the stitching, to reveal the fabric below. Continue within this motif, alternately stitching and cutting away, to reveal selected areas of the underlying fabrics.

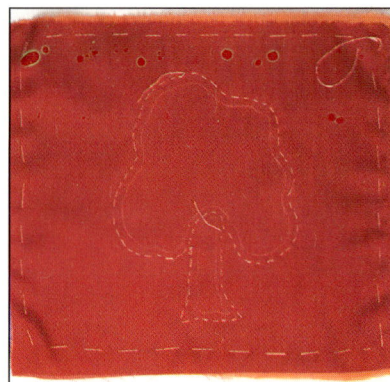

1 Cut three layers of fabric on the straight grain to the required full size, using dressmakers' carbon paper to mark the design on the top piece. Pin the pieces together, matching the grainlines. Baste, 1cm (⅜in.) out from the marked outer edge, around each shape that is to be removed.

2 With small sharp embroidery scissors, start to cut away the top layer of fabric, cutting 6mm (¼in.) inside the marked outline.

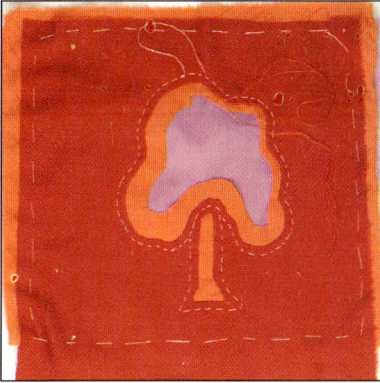

3 Turn this raw edge under and, using thread that matches the upper fabric, slipstitch in place through all layers, snipping curves as necessary. Continue cutting away, turning under and stitching until the shape is completed. Repeat steps 1 and 2, cutting through the second layer to reveal the third. Additional shapes may be applied within the cut-away area, using the turned-edge method.

This section of a quilt made by Elspeth Kemp shows a combination of reverse appliqué with turned-edge shapes, attached both by hand and machine.

Inlay

Inlay was known in the 19th century as mosaic work. At that time, it was usually made in felt, the shapes being cut out and stitched together invisibly to form a perfectly flat piece of work with solid areas of colour. During the late Victorian era and the early years of this century, inlay held a major place in ecclesiastical embroidery, being used for banners and altar frontals of brocade and velvet, with accompanying couching in gold cord covering the joins between the various inlaid fabrics. Today, although it is not often used, its most interesting advantage is that the technique produces a smoothness

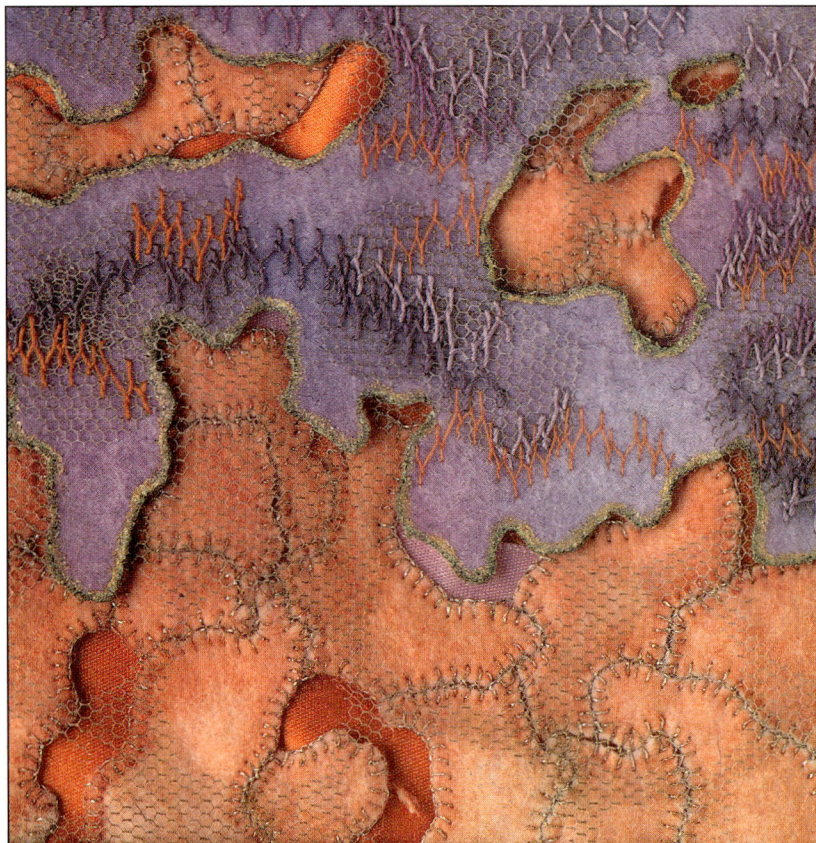

1 Mark your design on the right side of the main (background) fabric, using dressmakers' carbon paper or drawing around a template. Lay this on top of the fabric to be inlaid. Place the two fabrics on a cutting board and pin them both to the board to hold them firm. Using a sharp scalpel or craft knife, cut through both layers of fabric, following the marked outline. This will produce two sets of shapes which can be inlaid, one in the other.

For this unusually delicate piece of inlay work, Judy Hope has used painted and dyed felt, net and embroidery.

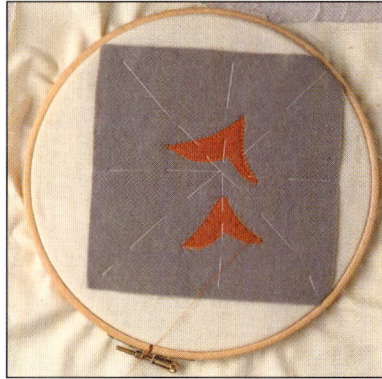

2 Traditionally, inlaid appliqué has no permanent backing, and the work can therefore be reversible. Pin and baste the pieces of fabric – main fabric and inlaid piece(s) to a temporary backing of brown paper (originally, parchment was used). The raw edges may be joined either by sewing them together and concealing the join with couched cord or thread, or by working a row of buttonhole stitch on both raw edges, interlocking the second row with the first. The stitching should not pierce the brown paper.

3 A modern method is to mount a backing of firm fabric in a frame, and then pin and baste the appliqué pieces in position. Either work feather stitching along the joins, catching in both edges and the backing, or replace the handstitching with machine zigzag. In this case, the finished appliqué has a backing and is therefore not reversible.

unobtainable with other types of appliqué, and in addition it can be made reversible if the pieces are not stitched on a backing.

The easiest fabrics to work with are those, such as felt, closely woven wool and painted or dyed interfacing, that do not fray. The type of design best suited to the technique is one containing bold shapes and without narrow strips, as the pieces of appliqué fit together like a jigsaw puzzle with the edges abutting one another. Although the finished appliqué was traditionally unmounted, a simpler way to work is to mount a backing in a frame, place the main background fabric on this and stitch the inlay pieces into the appropriate spaces.

Stained glass appliqué

Stained glass appliqué is so-called because it closely resembles the craft of that name. It is similar in some ways to inlay (see page 42) but in this case it is always mounted on a backing, and the bright, jewel-like pieces of coloured fabric are separated either by purchased bias binding or by a bias strip of dark, contrasting fabric, which represents the leaded divisions of church windows. In a design made up of straight-sided geometric shapes, ribbon can replace the bias strip. The allover type of design suitable for this method will need to be adapted and simplified, each area being outlined with a felt tip pen

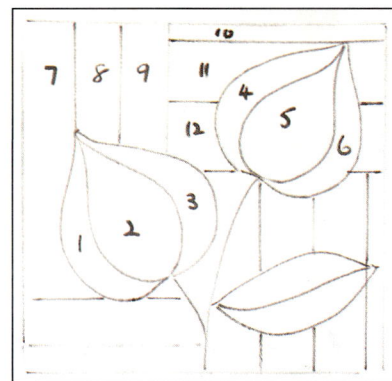

1 Transfer the design to a white or neutral background fabric, by tracing directly on the fabric or with dressmakers' carbon paper.

In this design of a face, pieces of satin bonded to the background are separated with wide satin machine stitching.

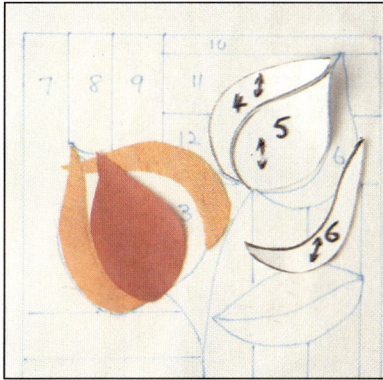

2 Cut a paper template for each section of the design; number the templates, as well as the corresponding areas on the original design, and mark the grain lines. Use the templates to mark the fabric pieces, matching grain lines. Cut out the shapes and either baste them in place on the background or fuse them, using the design as a placement reference.

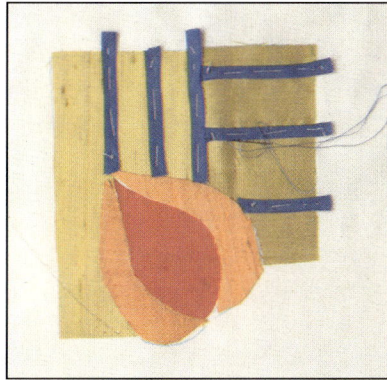

3 Fold under the long edges on each bias strip, pressing them to meet down the centre back. Cut the strips in lengths to fit the outlines of the appliqué shapes. Baste the lengths in place, covering the joins between the pieces already in position. Slipstitch along each edge of every strip, using matching thread and making sure that the stitches pass through all layers of fabric.

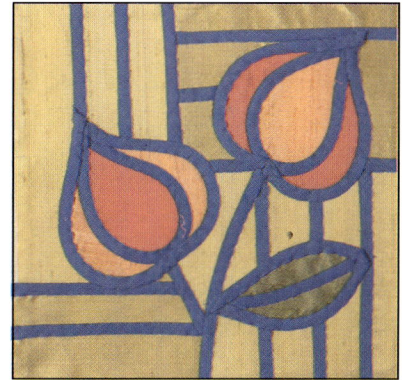

4 When stitching sharp curves, always sew the inner edge before proceeding to the outer. Where one strip runs to meet another, tuck the end under the continuous strip.

to accentuate the bold shapes. Make sure that there are no isolated outlines, but that all the lines interconnect and lead to the outside edges of the design, as in a piece of stained glass.

The choice of fabric is wide, but it is usual to select fabrics of a similar weight and type, in order to achieve a well coordinated design. For the bias strips, use a fine fabric, such as cotton lawn. Cut and join strips, making them twice the finished width. This should be appropriate to the design – 1cm (⅜in.) might be a suitable finished width for the strips on a large design, such as a wall hanging, while slightly narrower strips might be better for a smaller project.

For a quick alternative, the joins may be covered by wide satin stitch, worked by machine, the neatness of this approach making it ideal for items, such as window blinds or lampshades, through which the light shines.

Shadow appliqué

Shadow appliqué uses a variation of the stitch-and-cut method (see page 29) but in this case the fabric to be applied is placed beneath the transparent background fabric and the excess cut away. This method produces a very delicate impression, due to its use of transparent fabrics such as organdie, organza, voile, nylon or net. Pretty effects can also be obtained with shot organza and crystal nylon, which has a sparkly finish, while chiffon and georgette, although rather difficult to handle, have interesting potential. As the appliqué is stitched to the underside of the sheer fabric the result is mainly of muted tones.

Traditionally, only white fabrics have been employed, but more exciting effects can be achieved by using materials of different colours. This will produce alterations of hue; for example, a yellow cotton placed beneath a red organza will appear to be orange. Experiment with trimmings of fabric of different colours under a piece of net or voile, and you can explore the possibilities of exploiting the differences in colour density, as well as change of tone and hue. The soft tones of this technique make it a suitable medium for lingerie and pretty evening wear, scarves or wedding veils. Transparent soft furnishings, like lampshades and window blinds or lace curtains, can also be embroidered in this way.

As with most types of appliqué, designs for this method should be fairly bold in concept. Unless there is going to be some additional decorative stitching, it is necessary to divide the design into sections, rather like a stencil, with each area separated from its neighbour by a space.

Originally a hand sewing method, sewn with pin stitch, shadow appliqué can also be made by machine, using a narrow close zigzag stitch.

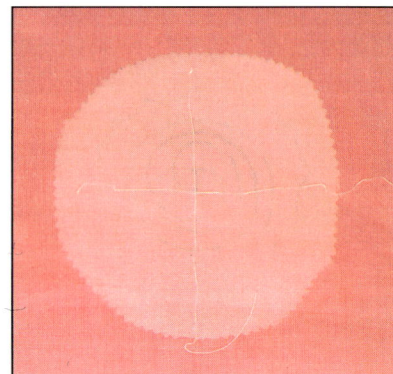

1 Transfer the design to the top, transparent fabric with a water-soluble fabric marker or dressmakers' chalk, using the direct tracing method. Mark very lightly.

Mount this fabric in a frame, then cut enough of the appliqué fabric to cover the design area completely and baste it in place underneath, making sure that the straight grains of the two pieces are aligned.

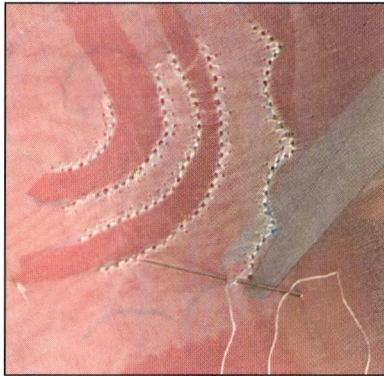

2 From the top, work pin stitch in fine thread, taking the stitches through both layers and stitching along the marked outlines around each shape. Remove the work from the frame and carefully cut away the excess fabric from underneath, cutting from the wrong side of the work and using sharp embroidery scissors.

If you are using a machine, baste the traced design over the two layers of fabric. Work narrow satin stitch or close zigzag through all three, then tear away the paper. Trim the excess fabric as for the hand method.

The same design shown in the steps has here been stitched by machine.

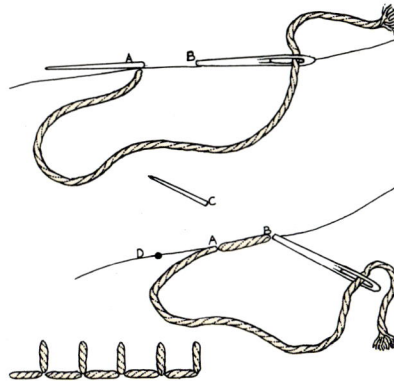

3 To work pin stitch, make a back stitch from A to B and bring the needle up again at A. Repeat the backstitch, this time bringing the needle up at C. Take the needle down at A and bring it up at D. Repeat the stitch, pulling the thread fairly tightly to form small holes.

Carrickmacross lace

From the Irish market town of that name, Carrickmacross lace is actually a net appliqué worked in a similar way to the shadow method, except that in this case the appliqué fabric is placed on top instead of beneath the background. Traditionally, these white-on-white designs were floral, simulating Brussels lace, but a contemporary approach might be to use coloured fabrics, which could be handpainted or dyed. A layer of fine linen or cotton or muslin is laid on nylon or cotton net, or silk tulle, and, as with the shadow method, the outline is stitched and the surplus trimmed away. The outline running stitch is then overcast to prevent fraying, and additional running stitches are worked through the net to link motifs or emphasize details.

Hawaiian appliqué

Hawaiian appliqué, which is traditionally quilted, is characterized by large-scale designs, in which a solitary motif radiates from the centre of the piece and reaches almost to the edges. The designs were taken from the shapes of the islands' fruits and flowers, but you can easily create your own motifs by folding and cutting paper to make patterns. One of the most popular Hawaiian motifs is the breadfruit design, but others, such as pineapple, prickly pear and sunflowers, are also used, mainly on panels, cushions and quilts. The quilting lines normally follow the outline of the appliqué shapes in contours.

Although it is a simple task to create your own designs, care should

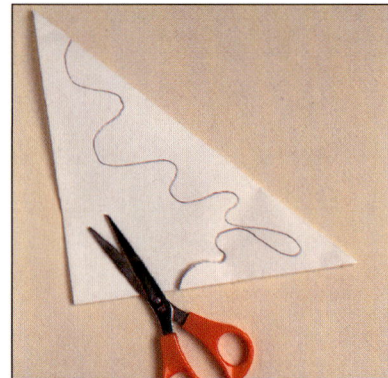

1 Take a square of firm paper, the size of the finished background, and fold it in half, then in half again. Make a diagonal fold, taking the corner at the centre of the paper to meet the corner with all the four corners of the original square. Take great care, when folding, to be as neat and accurate as possible. Draw the design on the paper triangle, as shown, and cut it out, cutting through all the layers.

Traditionally, Hawaiian appliqué uses only two colours – the background colour and that of the single piece of applied fabric – but in this panel by Hilary Stenning, featuring blue gentians, two more colours are added, to make the flower heads.

2 Trim the background and appliqué fabrics to the same size as the paper square, taking care to cut along the grainlines. Carefully fold and press the fabrics in exactly the same way as the paper.

Pin the paper pattern to the appliqué fabric, matching fold lines. Mark round the edge; remove the pattern, and cut out the design.

3 Pin and baste the appliqué piece to the background, matching grainlines and folds.

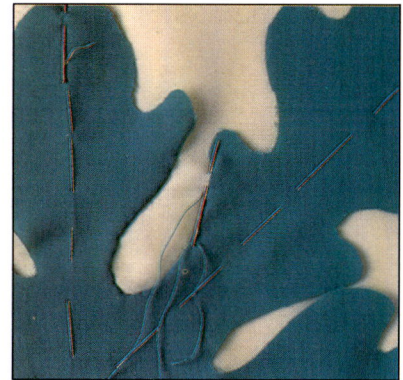

4 You will find it much easier to sew neatly if the prepared fabric is mounted in a frame. Use the turned-edge method to attach the design to the background, turning the hem as you go and snipping curves and points.

Place the appliquéd top fabric over a piece of thin batting, backed by a backing fabric; pin and tack the layers together, then quilt in lines following the design outline and spaced about 12mm (½in.) apart.

be taken that the scale is bold and there are broad curves; very acute points and sharp concave shapes should only be attempted when you are experienced at this method. The most satisfactory results are achieved by using fine cotton lawn or poplin for the appliqué, mounted on fabric of similar type. Springy synthetic fabrics are less easy to handle and should be avoided if possible. Experiments on a large scale could, however, include fine wool or needlecord, for items such as wallhangings or bedcovers. Hawaiian appliqué has traditionally been restricted to two plain fabrics, but there is no reason why the technique should not be adapted to combine more colours or printed fabrics. Choose strongly contrasting colours to accentuate the design.

Patchwork appliqué techniques

Although most forms of patchwork do not come within the category of appliqué, some techniques, such as Suffolk puffs (yo yo patchwork), clamshells and folded star, or crazy patchwork, incorporate the application of fabric shapes to a background fabric as opposed to piecing them together. Complete projects, such as quilts and cushions, may be created using these processes, or small sections may be integrated with other appliqué and embroidery methods for interesting pictures or wallhangings.

As with any type of design that relies for its effect on the fabrics used, care should be taken in their selection; in particular, examine the scale of the pattern, if printed material is chosen, and also the relationship between the tonal values of the various colours. Fabrics should not only complement the design aesthetically but they should also be suitable from a practical point of view.

Crazy patchwork (1, 2)

Crazy patchwork is similar to stained glass appliqué in that the fabric pieces completely cover the background. In this case, however, fabric scraps of almost any shape or size may be used. Iron-on interfacing may be substituted as a backing, so that instead of being pinned and tacked in place, ready for stitching, the patches can quickly be applied to the interfacing, as shown.

Using this technique, designs can be created that may range from intuitive and haphazard arrangements to more formal patterns of geometric pieces placed alongside one another. If you are making a very large piece, such as a curtain or quilt top, you may find it easier to make up squares and then join these into a large shape.

Traditionally, the raw edges were covered with herringbone or feather stitch; today, decorative open zigzag machine stitching may be used instead. The fabrics can be of any type and colour – provided the patches are applied to a backing fabric when you stitch over the raw edges, it is possible to mix, say, cottons and velvets – but the most successful designs are usually those using a limited range. A multi-coloured selection can be coordinated by using a single colour for the embroidery.

1 Cut a piece of iron-on interfacing the size of the finished design and lay it out, shiny side up. On this, arrange the pieces of fabric, with right sides up and slightly overlapping their raw edges. Pin the pieces, then press carefully, removing the pins as you proceed, to adhere the fabric to the interfacing.

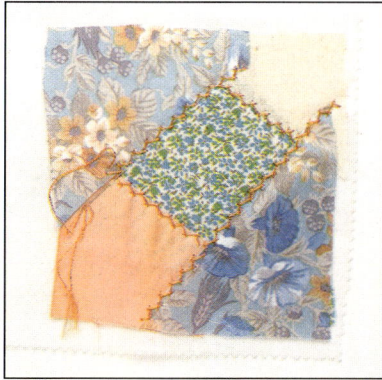

Suffolk puffs, or yo yo patchwork (3, 4)

Suffolk puffs are made from gathered circles of fine fabric, such as lawn or thin silk, and can be used to decorate soft furnishings or garments – they would look pretty scattered as a decoration on a child's party dress or bridesmaid's dress. Their resemblance to flower-shapes makes them an ideal addition to embroidered pictures of gardens or landscapes. They can be attached individually or joined together to form a whole fabric. Experiments can be made with different sizes and fabrics; the centres may be filled with beads, padding or contrasting material.

2 Add feather or herringbone stitch to cover the joins, or use machine zigzag or satin stitch. If the piece is likely to receive much wear, pin and baste a backing fabric to the work and stitch through all layers.

Machine stitching gives a quilted effect to an evening bag.

3 To make a Suffolk puff, cut a circle of fine fabric, approximately twice the diameter of the finished piece. Using a fine needle and thread, gather the edge, turning a narrow hem as you proceed. Pull the thread tight, to gather the stitches, and fasten off firmly. Flatten the circle so that the gathers are in the centre of the finished puff.

4 Either sew individual puffs to the selected background fabric, placing a few stitches at the centre of each, or join them in rows, sewing the edges together where they touch.

Clamshells

Clamshell patchwork, also known as shell or fish-scale, is actually an appliqué method, in which purchased metal or plastic templates are used to mark the shapes, which are then prepared and mounted on a backing fabric. It is appropriate for decorating cushions and small items, such as tea-cosies or table mats, or it can enhance the yoke or pockets of a garment. The orthodox method is for all the pieces to be cut to the same dimensions, but experiments with differing sizes and a variety of fabrics can produce interesting work. Clamshell shapes

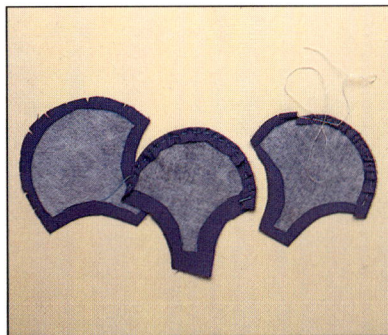

1 Using the template, mark as many clamshell shapes as are required for the finished work, marking the shapes on the dull (non-adhesive) side of the iron-on interfacing. Cut them out carefully, using small sharp scissors. Iron the interfacing shapes to the wrong side of the selected fabrics, making sure that the straight grain runs vertically down the centre of each shape and allowing a 6mm (¼in.) margin all around each shape.

2 Cut the shapes out, with a 6mm (¼in.) allowance around each. Turn the hem to the wrong side along the curved top edge of each shape, using the interfacing as a guide. Baste with small stitches, taking small notches out of the excess fabric if necessary.

3 Mount the backing fabric in a frame. Pin and baste the top row of shells, right side up, in a straight line and with sides touching. Pin and baste the second row over the first, staggering it as shown, to cover the raw edges. Continue with subsequent rows as required, until all the shell shapes are pinned in position. Slipstitch the curved edges neatly through all layers. Alternatively, use straight, zigzag, or decorative machine stitching. The bottom edge of the final row may be cut short and either hemmed or covered with a strip of fabric.

also have their uses on appliqué panels; to simulate fish-scales, roof tiles or petals, for example.

Traditionally, each clam-shaped patch was prepared by pinning a paper guide, the size of the finished patch, to the right side of the patch, turning down the top, scalloped curve to the wrong side, and basting it. The guide could then be used to prepare the next patch, and so on. Using iron-on interfacing, as shown here, is faster and makes it much easier to achieve a neat, accurate curve, though the interfacing stiffens the finished piece.

A mixture of batik and home-dyed fabrics have been used for this clamshell sample by Prue Dobinson, in which the scale of the clamshells varies, creating extra interest and a sense of movement.

Folded Star

Folded star (also known as Somerset) patchwork is a comparative newcomer to the appliqué and patchwork scene. It is composed of small folded triangles of fabric arranged to form star-shapes or kaleidoscopic circular patterns. These patterns can be used to make circular cushions, and individual triangles can also be used for border decoration or inserted in a seam. Fine fabric, such as cotton lawn, which will retain a crease when pressed, is the most satisfactory material to use for your first experiments (the folding uses a comparatively large quantity of fabric), but others may be tried for designs requiring a bold or large scale.

In this folded star design by Anna Griffiths succeeding rows are carefully placed so that the initial circle gradually evolves into a squared shape.

1 Cut a number of 5cm (2in.) squares of fabric (four are needed for the first row, eight – in a contrasting colour or pattern – for the second). Fold each in half lengthwise. Next, bring the corners of the folded edge to meet at the centre of the opposite edge. Press well.

2 Prepare a piece of firmly woven cotton for the backing by drawing on it a square or circle the size of the finished design. Using a ruler and pencil, mark diagonal, vertical and horizontal lines, as shown. Mount the fabric in an embroidery frame and, using the marked lines as a guide, arrange four triangles so that their points touch at the centre. Stitch along the raw edges by hand or machine, and attach each centre point with a small invisible stitch.

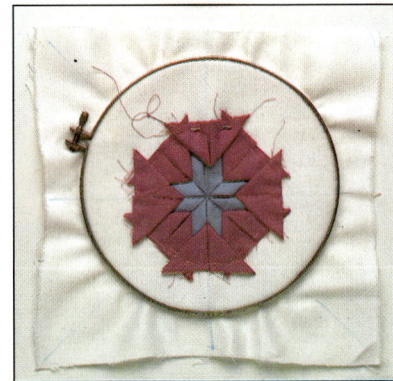

3 For the next row, add eight contrasting triangles, covering the raw edges of the first row and stitching as before. Sixteen triangles are needed for the next row and so on, each row radiating to form a pattern. This will produce a circular piece of appliqué, which can be inserted into a circle of fabric. The scale of the shapes may be altered, if desired, with larger triangles used towards the outside of the design.

Individual triangles can also be arranged as a border for edging soft furnishings or clothes.

CHAPTER FOUR

CREATIVE APPROACHES

Creating painted backgrounds

Paint may be added to an appliqué design, either at the beginning or as a finishing touch. This is one way of transforming an otherwise negative background space, helping to evoke the mood or atmosphere of a picture. Individual motifs may also be painted before they are applied to the background.

All-purpose fabric paints
These are suitable for any type of fabric. Pre-wash the fabric to remove any finishing, then mount it in a frame or tape it to your work surface with masking tape. Precise patterns can then be painted with a brush, using as little water as possible. For washes of diluted colour, wet the fabric before using a sponge or large brush to apply the paint, which will dry to a lighter colour.

Silk paints
These are very watery and are best used for translucent background effects or to create beautifully shaded fabrics for appliqué. For a more precise image, frame the fabric and outline each motif with gutta resist, a special dye-resistant barrier.

Transfer paints and crayons
These are suitable for synthetic fabrics only. The design is painted on paper and, when it is dry, the paper is placed over the fabric and ironed, transferring a mirror image.

Drawing on fabric
As well as fabric paints, there are various other ways of drawing on fabric. You may use ordinary permanent pens and felt tips, or products, such as transfer crayons, ball point paint tubes and fabric pens, that have been created specially for textile decoration.

Quilting, appliqué and painted fabric are combined in this sample piece by Sheila Cahn. Instead of scouring the shops for fabrics of the correct colour, it is often both simpler and cheaper to paint or dye plain fabric.

Spraying and spattering

In addition to sponging or brushing, the various methods of spraying or spattering give interesting textural effects. This type of painting is usually best accomplished during the early stages of a work, as it can be difficult to control. Mask areas that are not to be covered.

Toothbrush spattering

All-purpose or transfer paints are best for this method – silk paints may be used, but the spattering will tend to run. The work should be pinned or mounted in a frame, placed in either a horizontal or vertical position, or secured to the work surface with tape. Dip the tooth-brush into the undiluted fabric paint; hold it away from you with the head uppermost, and draw a piece of stiff cardboard or the blade of a knife towards you, across the bristles, directing the paint to the appropriate areas of the design.

Mouth spray diffuser

This little gadget produces a similar, grainy effect to the toothbrush spattering. In this case, the work should be mounted or pinned in a frame and placed vertically. Having diluted the paint to a milky consistency, place the mouthpiece of the diffuser in your mouth and the other end in the jar of paint. Keep about 15–20cm (6–8in.) away from the work; take a deep breath, and blow steadily and hard. This method may take a little practice.

Spray-guns

There are a number of models on the market, ranging from expensive airbrushes with compressors to reasonably-priced guns that work very successfully with aerosol cans of liquid airbrush propellant. Choose one with a container large enough to hold sufficient paint for the entire project. Tape the work to a flat surface. Carefully dilute the paint to a milky consistency, making sure that there are no lumps to block the nozzle. Hold the spray-gun about 15–20cm (6–8in.) from the design and, keeping your finger on the button, move it steadily in a series of smooth movements from side to side. Apply a light coat at first, then re-spray if necessary.

Using stencils (1, 2)

A stencil acts as a mask, preventing the paint from being applied to unwanted parts of the design. Other types of mask, through which paint can be sprayed or painted, provide a variety of negative images of different textures and patterns – rug canvas and wire mesh of various sizes give interesting effects; strips of masking tape will assist in the making of geometric designs. In all cases, if spraying or spattering, remember to cover the area beyond the perimeter of the stencil or mask with protective paper.

1 Draw or trace the design on stiff cardboard or self-adhesive film. Make sure that each shape is separate so that the stencil will hold together once the shapes are cut out – if necessary, simplify the design in order to achieve this. Place the design on a cutting board and, using a craft knife or scalpel, carefully cut out the shapes.

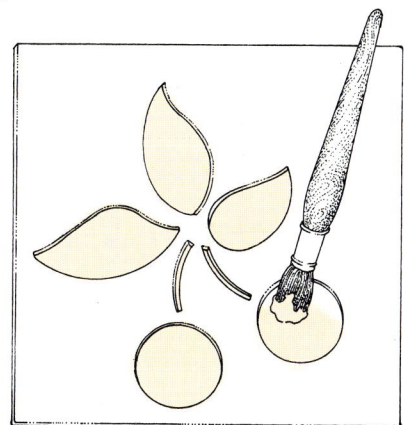

2 Apply undiluted fabric paint, preferably using a stencil brush with stiff bristles. Alternatively, spray or spatter the paint, using any of the methods discussed here.

This study by Jane Boot uses a sprayed and lino-printed background. Hand stitchery secures the appliqué, and some areas are cut away to reveal contrasting fabrics.

Dyeing fabrics for appliqué

Dyeing the fabrics and threads for an appliqué project is an ideal way to create unique and personal work. Follow the manufacturer's instructions, taking particular care to make sure that you have the right type of dye for the fabric. Weigh the fabric and measure out the dye used as accurately as possible so that you will be able to repeat the effect if necessary.

Cold-water dyes are the simplest type to use and are suitable for all natural fibres and viscose rayon fabrics, which should be pre-washed to remove any finishing. They are available in a wide range of colours, and these can also be mixed together for an even greater number of shades. Hot-water dyes should be used for most synthetic fibres, but they are not as colourfast as the cold-water variety. For tie-dye, it is best to choose strong colours for maximum effect and to remember that the strength of colour will be reduced considerably when the fabric has been rinsed and dried.

Follow the manufacturer's instructions carefully for mixing the dye, taking note of the amount of dye and water, in order that repeat shades can be made at a later date. Dissolve the powder thoroughly, so that no particles remain, and add the cold fix or salt and soda, stirring the solution at every stage. The contents of the dyebath should be used immediately as they will only remain stable for two or three hours after the salt and soda have been added. The fabric should be wetted before being immersed in the dye and then allowed to remain in the solution for the prescribed time. Stir occasionally, then remove and rinse thoroughly in cold water.

Plain and shaded dyeing

To achieve evenly dyed plain fabrics, choose a container large enough to accommodate the fabric uncreased. It is essential to use sufficient dye and water so as to completely submerge the fabric, which should then be stirred continuously. A smooth shaded or ombre effect can be made by holding one end of the fabric in both hands, immersing it in the dye and gradually withdrawing it. Repeat this process a number of times until you are satisfied with the colour, and do not allow the fabric to remain stationary.

Tie-dye techniques

Tie-dye techniques are found in folk art in various parts of the world. Very popular for clothing during the late 1960s, these methods of dyeing fabrics remain a useful way of creating subtle background interest for appliqué designs.

Marbling (1)
One of the simplest and most effective ways of creating a random, allover pattern, marbling is suitable for backgrounds and for applied fabrics. A marbled fabric can be re-tied after the first dye process and then re-dyed in another shade, if a multi-coloured effect is desired.

Folding and tying (2–6)
By folding and tying fabric before immersing it in the dyebath, you can produce a wide variety of patterns. If a fabric is folded in half and then bound, you will find that you have a mirror-image pattern after it has been dyed. Similarly, you can fold the fabric into four, or bind it diagonally or in accordion pleats, each method producing a different pattern.

It is a good idea to keep a notebook and record all the relevant details – the type of fabric, the exact quantity and mix of dye, the folding method, and the length of time spent in the dyebath – so that you will be able to achieve a near repeat, if you choose.

Areas of silk organza have been applied to a mottled, dyed background in this crocus panel, embellished with machine embroidery.

Marbling

Chevrons

Circular motifs

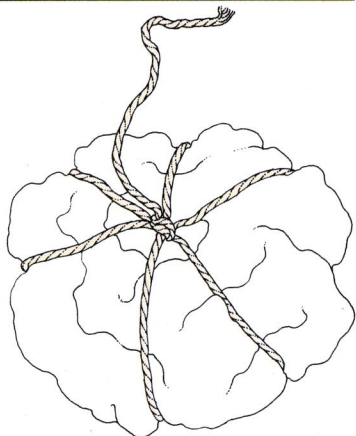

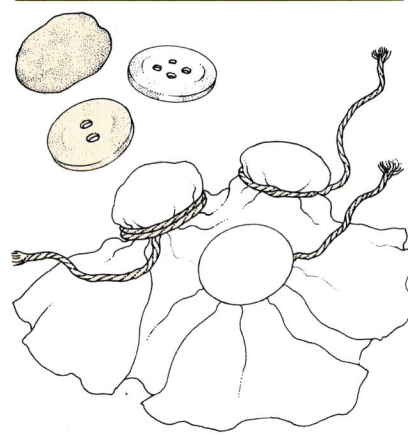

1 Crumple the fabric in your hand and bind it securely with strong thread, criss-crossing the surface. Fasten with a knot, leaving a tail with which to lower the bundle into the dyebath (tie the tail to a handle or loop it over the side). Wet the bundle, then immerse it in the dye and stir well. Check the depth of colour frequently and, when the desired colour is achieved, remove the bundle from the dyebath and rinse it. Untie it; rinse again; allow it to dry naturally, then iron it.

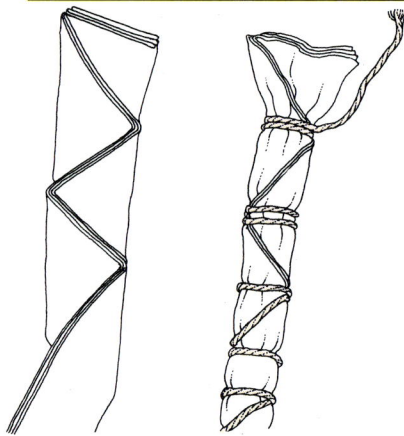

2 To make a chevron pattern, fold the fabric into accordion pleats, then pleat the fabric diagonally, as shown. Bind the fabric straight across to hold the pleats, and dye the bundle.

3 Circular motifs of a variety of types and sizes can be made by tying objects such as pebbles and buttons in the fabric. If you wish the motifs to fall in specific places, mark these areas lightly with a pencil before you start, as the fabric will become distorted as the tying proceeds.

Individual flowers

Circular sunburst

Mottling

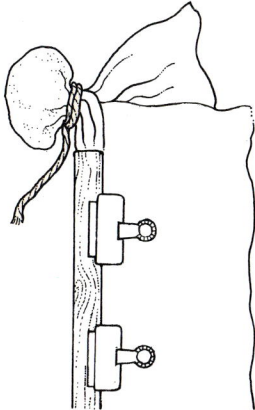

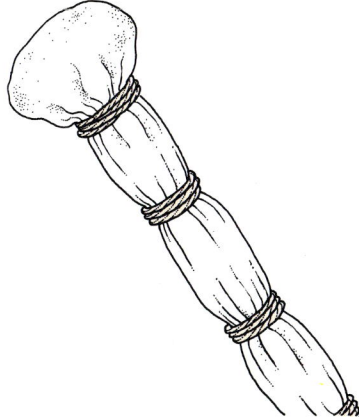

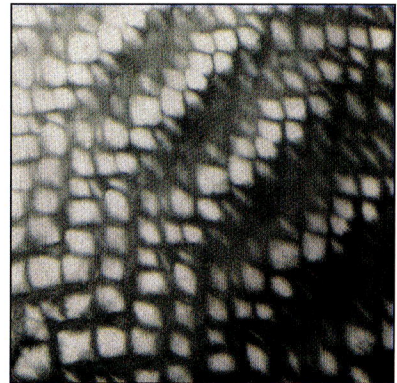

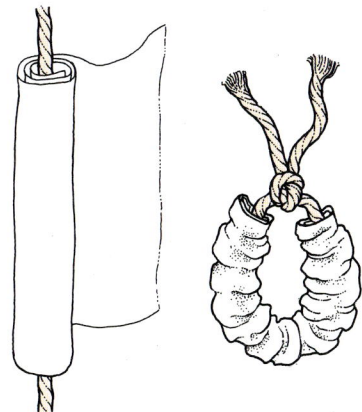

4 Individual flowers with stalks can be made by using a small button or stone for the head of each flower, then folding the fabric below the button/head. Use bulldog clips to clamp a wooden batten along the line of the fold when you dye the fabric.

5 A circular sunburst design can be produced by tying a large button or stone in the centre of a piece of fabric and then binding the remainder of the fabric at intervals, to create concentric circles.

6 You can achieve an attractive mottled effect by rolling a fine fabric, such as lawn or silk, over a piece of thick cord. Fold the roll in half and, holding the two ends of cord together, push the fabric up into a small bundle and tie the ends of the cord together.

Decorative stitches

Decorative stitches contribute another dimension to applique, help-ing to strengthen, define or soften outlines, or to bring movement, rhythm and direction to the design. Solid areas of texture can be produced, either on the applied shapes or on the background fabric; details that are too small or intricate to be carried out in fabric can be added in embroidery. Stitches may form decorative borders or conceal joins in the material, creating additional colour, pattern or texture.

It is not possible, within the limits of this book, to show how to make the many decorative stitches that may be used: what follows is just a list of suggestions that may lead you to creative ideas of your own. Most instructions show the conventional way of making a stitch, but once this has been mastered, you are free to experiment, adapting and modifying the stitches to make them more interesting. Try changing the scale and direction – work stitches haphazardly, or use varying thicknesses and types of yarn. Some stitches can overlap the edge of the appliqué, or encroach onto the background, softening the edges and helping to integrate the two surfaces.

Circular motifs are here emphasized with buttonhole, cretan and herringbone stitches.

Line stitches

Stitches may be categorized in many ways, but one obvious – and very useful – group consists of those which form lines. These include stitches such as couching, stem, chain, running, and back stitch, all of which can be used to emphasize and outline a piece of applied fabric.

Couching can be done in the conventional manner, with a yarn thick enough to conceal the join between the two fabrics. A more decorative approach might involve fly, detached chain or irregular stitches couching down the base thread.

Stem stitch can be worked in a single line or as close multiple rows. If two parallel lines are stitched, they can be whipped or laced together, forming a wide border.

There are many different types of chain stitch, including whipped, twisted, coral, double, broad, open and rosette. Each has its own particular quality and if you experiment you will develop many different ideas for use with various appliqué methods.

Above *Based on an exploded design, the raw edges of this line stitch sample are covered with couching, whipped and laced running stitches, and zigzag, open, twisted and rosette chains.*

Right *A variety of embroidery stitches are used to accentuate the appliqué shapes of this satin waistcoat by Nora Doerfel.*

Border stitches

When worked conventionally, border stitches form a wide decorative band. They can also be stitched more freely, creating a transition between the appliqué and the background fabric. In the past, the raw edges of appliqué shapes were secured almost exclusively with buttonhole stitch, but as well as the orthodox buttonhole stitch there are a number of variations, including closed, crossed, up-and-down, tailor's and knotted, any or all of which can be subjects for experiment. Herringbone and cretan stitch are both extremely versatile, creating varied and interesting textures. They can be worked in an open fashion, forming a neat zigzag edge; a more fluid effect can be obtained by stitching haphazardly, merging the appliqué with the background fabric. Although worked in a similar way, closed cretan and closed herringbone appear quite different, and make a solid band of stitchery. Feather stitch and double feather have traditionally been employed to conceal the edges of crazy patchwork, but they can be used with other methods for a highly decorative effect.

Filling stitches

Filling stitches, including satin, long and short, Bokhara and Rumanian couching, entirely cover the surface, producing a smooth textured effect. Open laid-work fillings very often form a trellis pattern, allowing the fabric underneath to be seen, while single unit stitches can be either scattered or massed together.

Satin stitch and long and short stitch are found in the embroideries of many lands, particularly in China. They can be used to define form and create movement on a plain fabric or provide contrasting texture to a background area – their beauty is dependent on the skill of the embroiderer in creating a smooth silky surface. Attention should be paid to the tension and to the direction of stitching: when filling spaces, satin stitch should be worked diagonally, but for a solid line securing a piece of appliqué it may be stitched at right angles to the edge of the fabric. Long and short stitch is often used for shading large areas, but for appliqué it could serve to cover the raw or turned edge. The lattice effect of open laidwork fillings could transform an applied shape, lightening or darkening the tonal value, and adding pattern. The base stitches may be taken through the background fabric and secured with either contrasting or matching thread. Single unit stitches, which include French knots, detached chain, detached wheatear, fly stitch, seeding and blocks of straight stitches, are effective either massed together to cover an area completely, or as a lighter texture, scattered over the surface of both the appliqué and the background.

These are just some of the embroidery stitches that can decorate and embellish your appliqué designs. There are, of course, many others to choose from, all of which will help to add interest in terms of colour, pattern and texture.

In this landscape by Sheila Dewick, layers of translucent fabric have been combined and edged with cretan stitch. Fly stitches in the foreground build up the thick texture of the hedgerow.

Decorative machine stitches

Decorative machine stitches will not only hold the appliqué firmly in place but will also add individuality to a piece of work. Some stitches will impose themselves strongly on a design, emphasizing an outline. Alternatively, the stitch can be made to meander or encroach on the background fabric, disguising the hard edge of the appliqué, so that one fabric appears to merge into the other. Before embarking on machine embroidery, it is essential to study the manufacturer's handbook so that you are fully conversant with the working of your machine.

Ordinary cotton and polyester threads (if specified by number, in No. 50 weight) can be used for machine embroidery. Specialist machine embroidery threads (Nos 30, 40 and 50) are ideal and, in addition, come in shaded varieties. Some contain metallic fibres, which can add sparkle to luxury items.

Automatic stitches

Normal machining for straight, zigzag and automatic patterns requires a presser foot to be attached, enabling the fabric to be automatically fed under the needle by the feed-dog below. The feed dogs pass the fabric straight under the needle, making it less manoeuvrable, and for this reason, designs formed by straight lines and shallow curves are the most suitable. The effect tends to be formal and precise, giving a neat and immaculate edge to an appliqué motif.

A corded edge can be made by attaching a braiding or embroidery foot, which has a hole through which a cord is threaded. This is covered with close satin stitch. A braiding foot can also be used with a more open zigzag or some automatic patterns, in order to couch down a variety of thick yarns, giving a textured outline.

Built-in automatic patterns have different characteristics – some have a delicate lacy effect that can be used for attaching ribbon or lace appliqué on garment sections, such as collars, cuffs and yokes. Lingerie and baby-wear would also benefit from this treatment. The more geometric type of pattern can be used on sports and menswear, or to attach bold shapes to soft furnishing items, such as cushions.

Free machining

This technique has been likened to drawing with a needle and thread. The stitching has a spontaneity and freedom that can soften the outlines of appliqué motifs, helping to integrate them with the background fabric. It is essential to frame up the work correctly in an embroidery hoop (see page 15). The presser foot is removed and the feed dogs lowered (some machines have a special cover plate instead). This will allow the fabric to be moved in any direction. Plenty of time should be allowed for practice, and you should make a number of samples before embarking on a project.

This experimental piece by Prue Dobinson combines automatic and free machine embroidery, worked on a sprayed background.

Manipulating fabrics

Some of the most exciting effects can be achieved by manipulating fabrics, thereby creating new textures and shapes for use as backgrounds or for applied areas. The best way to find how individual fabrics can be manipulated, and the effects that can be achieved with different weaves and fibres, is to conduct a series of small-scale experiments.

You will find that pliable fabrics, such as chiffon, georgette, fine wool and crepe, drape well and will successfully gather and ruche into soft folds, but they are not so satisfactory for sharp pleats. On the other hand, crisp fabrics, such as poplin, linen, silk organza and taffeta, do not drape, but can be pleated and tucked very precisely for interesting linear effect.

Fraying

One decorative approach is to use the fraying qualities of a fabric to create feathery effects and changes of texture, or to soften the outline of a piece of applied fabric. The edges of tweeds, muslins, linens and loosely woven furnishing fabrics can be fringed to expose interesting warp or weft threads; shot silk is composed by combining two colours – one for the warp thread and one for the weft – so fraying this on both edges will produce an interesting effect. Sometimes the individual threads themselves can be untwisted and combed out.

Openwork effects

The creation of openwork effects, using similar fabrics to those that fray successfully, is another challenge for the inventive embroiderer. The warp and weft threads of loosely woven fabrics can be pulled apart to make holes; these may be stitched to retain the effect, as in pulled work, or applied to a contrasting background to introduce pattern or texture. The threads of closely woven materials are less easy to distort in this way; in this case, holes may be punched, cut or slashed. These can be backed with another fabric or threaded with strips of material, ribbon or yarn. Reverse appliqué can be adapted in an inventive fashion, with unusual fabrics, beads or sequins revealed in the cut-out areas.

In this five-panel landscape, Prue Dobinson has created many different effects by ruching, gathering and manipulating fabrics. Cretan stitch secures some areas.

Gathering and ruching

Gathered fabrics may be used as a textured background on wall-hangings or incorporated in appliqué panels. The gathers can be arranged precisely, in rows, to form an effect similar to that used for smocking; or the stitching can be more random, producing an irregular surface. A smocking machine can be used to gather small pieces of fine fabric, which can then be shaped into appliqué shells or flowers. If strips of fabric are gathered on one edge or lengthwise along the centre, frills of different types can be made; a ruched, scalloped edging will result if you gather a row of tiny stitches in zigzag formation along a narrow length of fine material. Shapes, such as the circles used in Suffolk puffs, may also be gathered, forming individual motifs that can be stitched to a background to simulate the effect of flowers or to create areas of texture.

Pleats and tucks

Pieces of pleated fabric may be stitched to appliqué panels or to soft furnishing items such as cushions – they can be made of different widths, formed either by hand or machine, pressed precisely into ridges or left unpressed for a softer effect. Lines of small tucks worked in groups can be used to depict the natural lines of landscape, ripples on a pond or architectural features: as always, your own observations will suggest ideas, and it may help if you keep a notebook with you and jot down possibilities as and when they occur to you.

Moulding fabric

Some fabrics, such as linen, scrim and hessian (burlap), are treated by the manufacturers with a finishing. If these fabrics are dampened, crumpled and pinned to a board in folds, bumps or ridges and allowed to dry, they will retain the shaping. Buttons, bottle-tops and similar items can also be used as a base over which to mould fabrics. These can subsequently either be used as a background or cut out and stitched to an embroidered surface.

If you saturate an absorbent fabric with wallpaper paste, PVA glue or a weak solution of plaster of Paris, you will be able to form rigid shapes suitable for wallhangings and panels.

A seascape panel by Sheila Dewick combines gathered with ruched fabrics, some with singed edges. These contrast with the smoothness of fabric-covered card.

Sealing the edges of fabric

For experimental pieces of textural and three-dimensional appliqué, the edges of fabric can be treated in several ways to prevent fraying and, in some cases, to stiffen them. Edges can be sealed with fabric glue, carefully and sparingly applied with a fine brush or a toothpick; another way is to singe the edges by holding the fabric near the flame of a lighted candle. This method should only be used with fabrics woven from natural fibres, as some synthetics flare dangerously – have a bowl of water at hand to dowse the burned edge. Fabric stiffener, sold for treating roller blinds, can be sprayed on most fabrics, which will then not fray when cut into shapes. Strips of fabric or ribbons can be rolled round a pencil or piece of wooden dowel and sprayed to create loose curls suitable for attaching to garments or embroidered panels.

Appliqué with other embroidery techniques

Traditionally, appliqué has been used as a skill in its own right or has played a significant role in the craft of patchwork and quilting. Indeed many patchwork pieces of the past contained areas of appliqué as centrepieces between the geometric patterns, and Persian appliqué motifs were sometimes stitched to a pieced background. Quilting has long been widely used, not only for motifs, coverlets and cushions, but also for warm and fashionable garments and accessories such as bags.

Apart from these traditional combinations, one of the most significant changes in contemporary needlework to evolve during recent years is the combining of several different embroidery techniques in a single piece of work. Appliqué, in particular, is one of the methods that lends itself to being combined with all types of work that use fabric and thread. Thus, surface stitchery can be added to areas of fabric that have been applied to give contrasts in colour or pattern. Padded areas of firm material or leather combine well with canvaswork – they should be attached firmly before the canvaswork stitches are made.

The other counted-thread methods of embroidery – cross-stitch and Assisi work, pulled- and drawn-thread work – do not at first glance lend themselves to embellishment with applied fabrics, but experiments can be made with fabrics of different types. Sheer materials, such as organza, chiffon or net, could add a muted effect to soften the surface tone on embroidered pictures or panels. In the case of pulled-work or drawn-thread work, a contrasting material can be applied to the underside to show through the holes. Cutwork and broderie anglaise projects can benefit from similar treatment. Metal thread embroidery has often, in the past, incorporated areas of silver or gold kid leather, padded over felt. This is not the only option – fabrics of all kinds can be laid down and stitched over with couched threads, or areas of purl can be combined with manipulated or ruched fabrics.

If you are willing to experiment with different ideas and techniques, there are few barriers, and by combining appliqué with other types of embroidery you will bring a fresh approach to your work.

Right *Suffolk puffs, placed face down, have been applied to a freely smocked, gathered background, in this work by Doreen Brewster.*

Far right *Free-standing appliqué ferns and leaves have been combined with a pulled work background and a machine quilted surround to create* Fern House at Kew Gardens.

Right *Machine zigzag has been used to quilt and add texture to this sample by Sheila Cahn.*

Incorporating other textile techniques

If you are conversant with other techniques, such as lacemaking, tatting, knitting, crochet or weaving, any of these may be used for appliqué, either alone or combined with applied fabrics and embroidery. Pieces of handmade textile might serve as backgrounds; they might be manipulated into folds and gathers, or they could be attached flat. Modern knitting machines also offer the opportunity to create exciting textures and patterns for possible inclusion in a design. For dress decoration, handmade lace and tatting can, of course, be applied to blouses and lingerie, whereas weaving is a suitable medium for making textiles to decorate household items such as cushions. Embroidered pictures, however, present most scope for these combinations. The experimental use of different media can combine various types of yarn in one piece of work; the scale of the stitches or weave can be altered, and additions such as beads may be incorporated. Small areas of texture or pattern can be knitted or woven; for example, strips can form the strata for a landscape, and flower motifs can be produced from crochet or lace for a garden picture. Because of the elasticity, particularly of knitting, larger shapes can be ruched, pleated or gathered to form an area of texture. Some knitting stitches, such as cables and bobbles, are particularly textural, while weaves can include knots and fringing; random textile shapes can be achieved by gradually increasing and decreasing the width of the piece.

Handmade fringes and braids can add a finishing touch to many types of project. These additions may be fashioned from ribbon, wool and cotton yarns, or even from torn lengths of fabric. Braids suitable for applying as edgings, or for use as bag and purse straps, belts and ties, can be made from the rouleaux – or fine tubes of fabric – that are used for narrow strip appliqué. These are also suitable for making loops, fringes or tassels or for decorative hanging effects. Tassels are a versatile trimming and can be created to embellish items such as the corners of an appliqué cushion or the bottom of a wallhanging. Although most handmade tassels are produced from yarn such as wool, it would be an innovative idea to experiment with fabrics that harmonize with those of the main project.

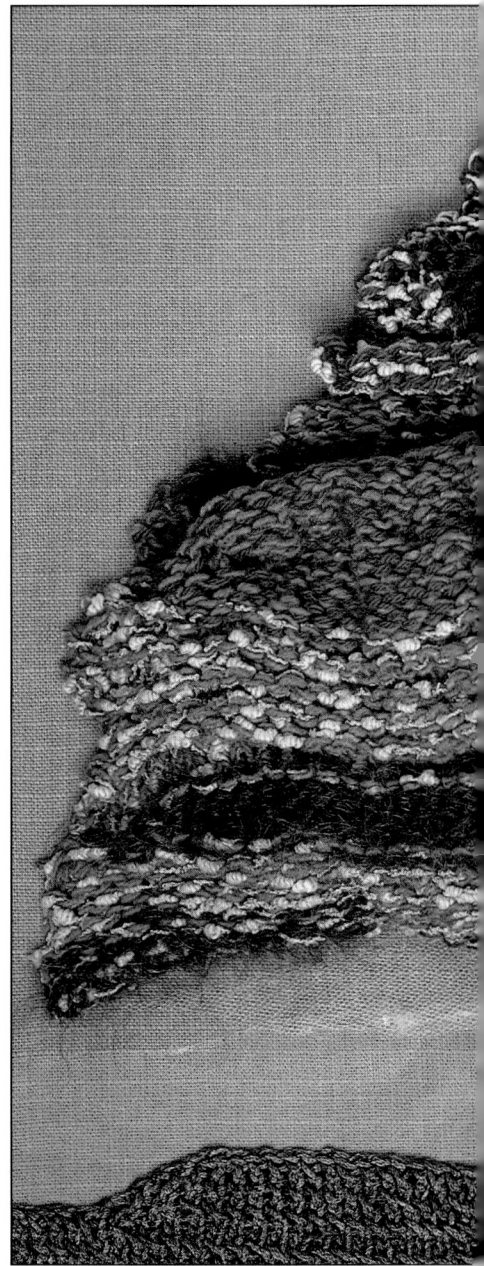

In this unusual knitted tree by Anna Griffiths, a variety of yarns are combined for maximum textural effect, and the motif is stitched to a fabric background.

Ribbons, braids and lace

Ribbons, braids and lace have been used for centuries for the embellishment of garments. Today there are many different types to choose from, many of them woven from synthetic fibres which, even though they may look delicate and attractive, will withstand frequent washing and ironing.

Whether you are adding decoration to a ready-made article, or are designing a project from the beginning, ribbon and lace appliqué is simple and quick to do. This type of treatment may be used with beautiful effect for special occasions such as weddings – a bridal dress with matching head-dress and veil can be trimmed with decorative bands and ribbon roses, with accompanying bridesmaids' dresses and head dresses similarly enhanced. Evening wear lends itself to velvet, satin or lurex ribbons. Jacquard ribbons and braids can also trim accessories of every type – belts, purses and bags, as well as decorations on shoes or hats.

Baby wear presents scope for appliqué, with the very narrow ribbons now available being ideal for delicate treatment on christening robes, cot quilts or nursery accessories. Contemporary children's wear often demands a bolder approach, which could be achieved with bright stripes and fancy pictorial ribbons.

Applying bands of colour is a quick and pretty way of introducing individuality to bedlinen. Hard-wearing, colour-fast polyester is the most suitable for coordinating sheets, pillow-cases and continental quilt covers; towels may be given a touch of luxury with wide satin ribbon. Cushions allow for plenty of freedom of design, with ribbons, braids and lace chosen for different effects, depending on the surrounding colours and textures of the rest of the interior design scheme.

Besides using ribbons and braids solely for functional articles, they can also create interesting effects on pictures and wallhangings, providing a wealth of different textures and surfaces – they can be formed into loops and fringes, pleated into geometric shapes or cut up and manipulated into textural areas. For stained glass appliqué (see page 44), narrow ribbon can divide the areas of the design, replacing the conventionally used bias seam binding.

As with fabrics and threads, it is a good idea to build up a collection of ribbons and braids. Even short lengths can prove useful, adding just the right texture or colour to a project.

Applying ribbons and braids

Ribbon appliqué requires little skill and is quick to do, especially by machine, as both edges are finished and require no further treatment. Braids, ribbons and lace can all be stitched down in a number of ways to create different effects. The most usual method is to baste the length in place along the edges, using a fine needle and thread. (Pins should be avoided if you are applying satin ribbon, as they tend to leave pin-holes.) Fusible web, especially that which is sold in narrow widths, is a very useful alternative way of positioning the ribbon prior to stitching.

Machine stitch along both edges, always in the same direction, so as not to distort the ribbon. If you are attaching several rows, these should all be stitched in the same direction. As an alternative to straight machine stitching, an open zigzag can be used; very narrow ribbons can either be couched down with a wide zigzag stitch criss-crossing the entire width, or, if you have one, you can use a twin needle attachment. Ribbons and laces with decorative edges and double-edge broderie anglaise may in some instances be attached with one line of stitching down the centre of the length, while you can give added interest to plain ribbons if you use automatic embroidery

Satin ribbon and strips of fabric with frayed edges were attached to this cushion with decorative machine stitching.

In this wallhanging by Diana Walker, ribbons have been used both for the Suffolk puff rosettes and the streamers.

stitches to hold them in place. Unless your machine has a special braiding foot, velvet ribbons and heavily patterned braids should be stitched using a zipper-foot, which will prevent the pile or texture from being crushed. If you prefer to sew by hand, use tiny stab stitch or hemstitching.

The inventive needlewoman will be able to create different variations on the conventional methods of attaching ribbons and braids. A row of gathers along one edge making a frilled effect provides a pretty trim for lingerie, babywear or blouses. Shell edging is a delicate alternative made by gathering a zigzag row of stitches that traverse the width of the ribbon. Some ribbons are difficult to manipulate, but others can be shaped into accordion or box pleats; folded and pressed into zigzags and triangles, they create interesting geometric and linear designs for the decoration of soft furnishings and linen or for clothes.

Braids may be formed with narrow ribbon or other trimmings. It is best to use those of the same width and weight so that the braid will be even. As these are flexible, they can be applied in cases where ordinary ribbon appliqué would not be possible, around curved shapes, for example, such as collars or circular cushions. They are also invaluable for straps for evening bags and purses, for ties and narrow belts. Shoulder straps for evening dresses and lingerie can also be fashioned in this way.

Ribbon flowers

Ribbon flowers have traditionally adorned hats for special occasions and in the past were used for corsages on the bodices of the gowns of Edwardian and Victorian ladies. There are, however, many other uses to which they can be put today. Pretty, feminine, soft furnishings can be enhanced with small roses or with carnations made of ribbon with pinked edges; short lengths of lace and ribbon may be gathered to form rosettes suitable for decorating a garment or an appliqué picture. Wedding fashions can incorporate different types of flower. A bridal headdress, such as a circlet or tiara, may be made entirely of ribbon roses or tiny rosebuds can be scattered over the dress or veil. Velvet and lurex ribbon flowers make attractive additions for evening dresses, bags and belts.

Right Children's wear is an ideal candidate for decoration with washable polyester ribbons, attached with wide zigzag stitch. The nursery print is stitched with straight machining.

Far right This sample shows a variety of different approaches to pleating and ribbons.

Right A shell edging and gathered ribbons make attractive additions to evening wear.

Far right This experimental piece uses sequin waste and lurex mesh, threaded with narrow ribbon and braid.

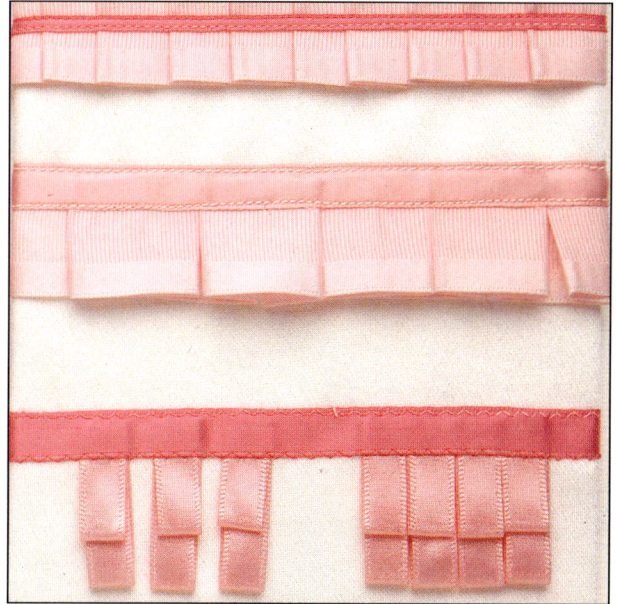

Beadwork

A theatrical, lavish effect can be conveyed by the addition of beadwork to a design. Attaching beads, spangles or sequins to evening wear, bags or belts is a simple task, but it immediately lifts the article into the couture class. Book-covers and fabric-covered boxes also benefit from this treatment, as can appliqué panels or wallhangings.

Beads come in many forms – they may be of glass, plastic, china or wood and they range in size from tiny seed pearls to large wooden varieties. Some are faceted and round, others smooth and long, pendant or lozenge-shaped. Sequins and spangles, too, are available in many colours and shapes. The most usual are the small round cup or disc type with a central hole. Specialist shops also stock sequins in the form of flowers, leaves, and stars as well as geometric shapes. Embroidery stones are different from beads in that they have a flat underside; some have holes for thread while others may need to be mounted, glued or sewn with covering stitches. Shisha (or mirror) glass requires a special method of application and makes an interesting addition to a design.

The most successful beadwork designs are those in which the beads or sequins are massed together, perhaps forming the focal point of a piece of work, or gradually diminishing in number from a cluster to a scattering. Because beads and sequins are inherently eyecatching and reflect the light, they will dominate a design as well as producing texture and pattern. For this reason, they tend to form a natural focal point of a design and should be used with care – if the intended focal point is elsewhere, a group of beads may weaken the effect.

If formal patterns are made, the beads should be sewn close together over an area, with attention paid to the direction in which they are laid; a design can look very weak if they are sparsely scattered.

Beads can be bought either loose or threaded on strings, as used for tambourwork. They can add lustre and richness to a design, but should be used with discretion, or they may overwhelm it.

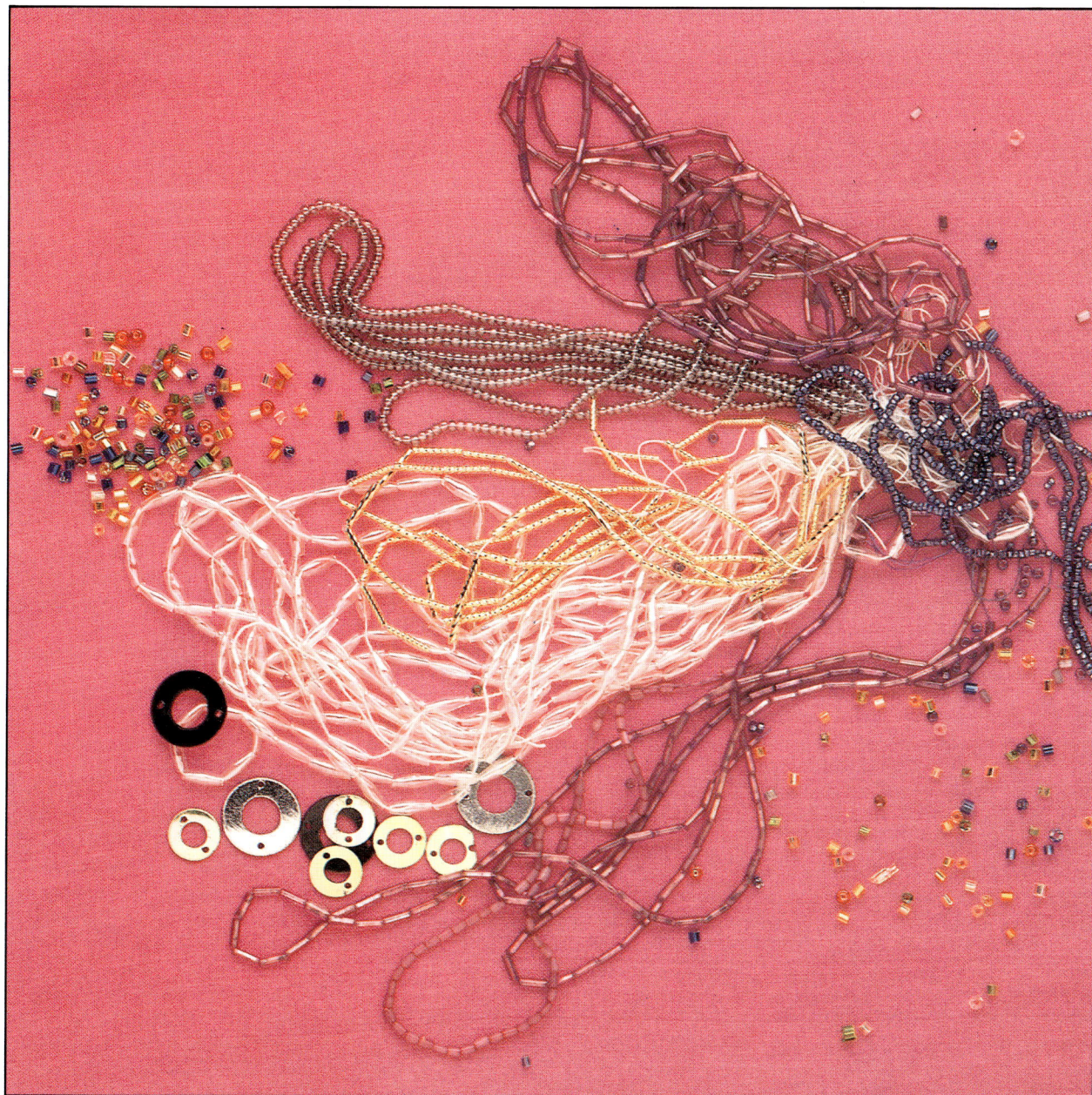

Attaching beads

Background fabrics for beadwork should be firmly woven, and it is essential that the fabric is mounted in a frame. If lightweight fabric, such as chiffon or organza, is used, it may be necessary to back the work with a slightly more substantial supporting material, such as fine lawn. This is cut away when the beading is finished.

Professional beadworkers use vanishing muslin as a supporting fabric. On completion of the design, a hot iron is applied to the back of the work; this causes the vanishing muslin to disintegrate and it can then be brushed away.

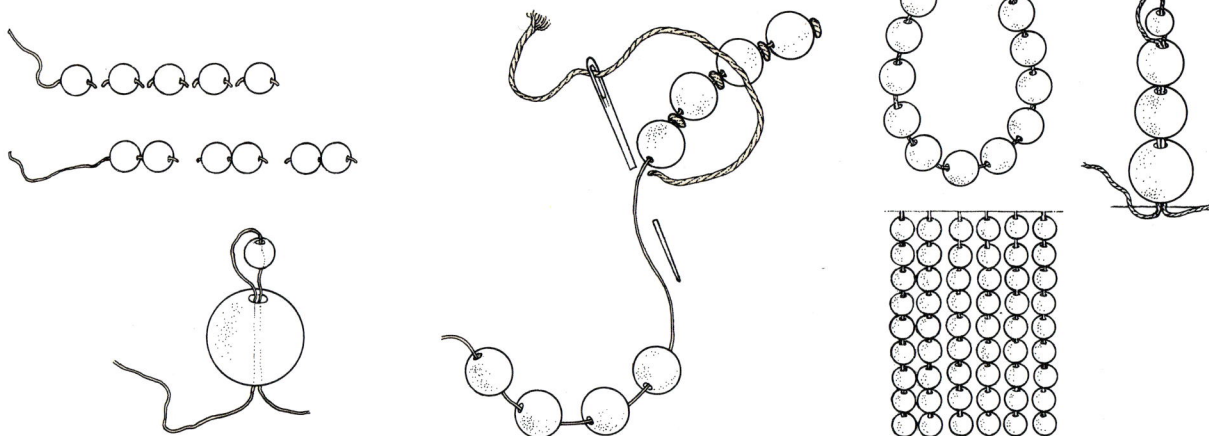

1 To attach beads singly, secure with a single stitch through the hole; to attach them in twos, secure with a single stitch through both beads. A large bead can be secured by using a smaller one to prevent the thread from pulling through.

2 To couch beads in rows, thread the required number on sewing thread and lay them on to the line of the design. Using a second needle and thread, take a tiny stitch across the row of beads, between every bead or every two or three beads, depending on the size of the bead, the strength of the fabric and the desired effect.

3 To sew a bead loop, pick up several beads (preferably an odd number) on the thread and re-insert the needle into almost the same spot on the fabric. If this process is reproduced many times a thickly encrusted texture will evolve.

Stalks can be made by threading three or four beads and taking the needle back into the same hole, passing again through all except the top bead.

Bead fringes or hanging tassels may be made in a similar fashion, using a greater number of beads.

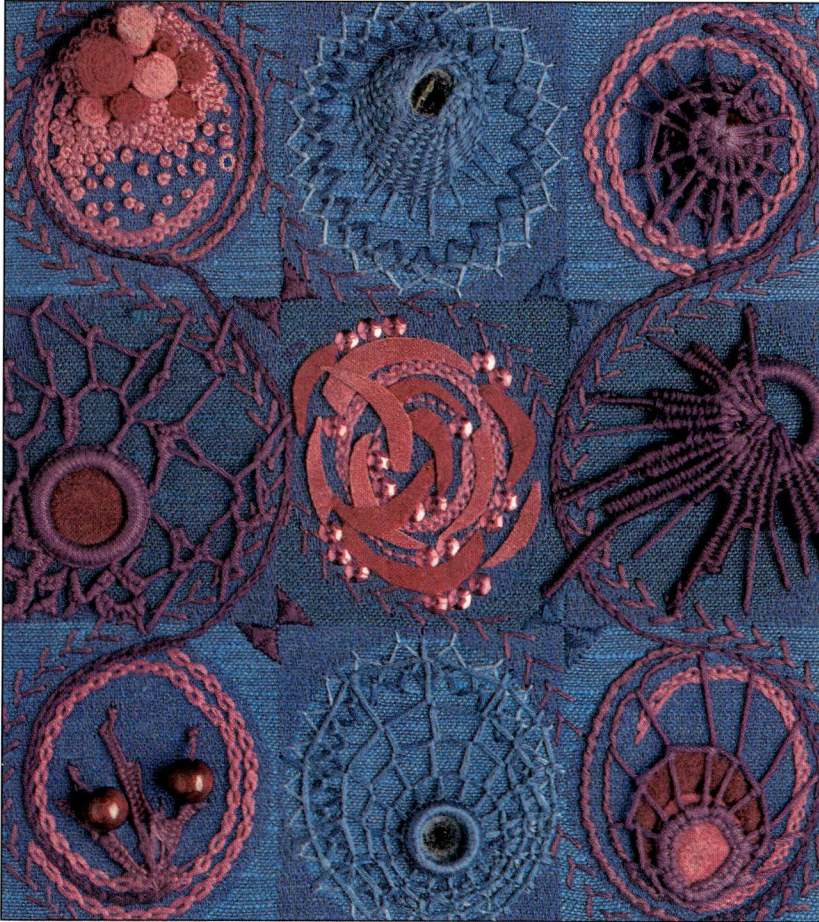

This sample produced by Margaret Horton on chequered fabric displays a wide variety of methods of attaching beads, jewels and curtain rings.

In some cases, you will find that your beads are already on a string, and can simply be couched in position. If they are loose, you will require a beading needle for tiny beads; others can be attached using any needle fine enough to pass through the hole. There are many ways of sewing beads to a fabric – either singly, in twos or threes, in rows, or in loops or fringes. Choose thread that tones with either the background or the overall colour of the beads. Draw it through a block of beeswax before you begin beading: this will smooth the thread and help it to retain its strength.

Sequins (1)

Sequins can be incorporated very successfully into appliqué designs for clothes and pictures. They may be either cup-shaped or flat, in which case the reverse side will feel slightly rough, where the hole was punched through. Take care when attaching sequins to work from the bottom of the design upwards, so that the row will lie smoothly.

Attaching jewels and stones (2)

Some jewels, including imitation and semi-precious stones, already have holes drilled through them to facilitate their attachment. In this case, they may be sewn in place with a beading needle and strong thread. Those without holes need different treatment: they may be glued to the surface with a rubber-based adhesive, or held in place by one of the methods shown here.

Shisha glass (3, 4)

Shisha (or mirror) glass embroidery involves the stitching of small pieces of mica to a background. This technique comes originally from India, Pakistan and Baluchistan, where it is used in combination with embroidery stitches for clothes and for decorative use on occasions such as festivals and weddings. As with other types of bead embroidery, the background fabric should be firm and closely woven in order to support the weight of the glass, particularly if a large number of pieces is being used on a garment or hanging. The small circles of silvered glass do not have holes in them, and may be attached in the same way as jewels and stones. The traditional method, however, involves a type of buttonhole stitch worked over glass.

Incorporating other decorative items

Besides the conventional decoration of fabric with beads, jewels and shisha glass, there are many other items which can be applied to an embroidered or appliqué piece. These may range from shells, pebbles, driftwood, feathers and seeds to machine-made components, such as washers, nuts and curtain rings. As most of these do not have holes to stitch through, they may be attached either by using an adhesive or by one of the fabric-and-thread methods described.

Sequins

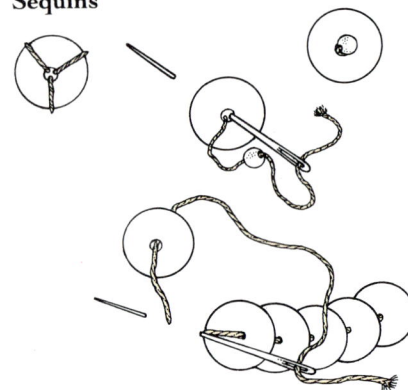

1 Individual sequins may be attached with two or three straight stitches, taken across and through the central hole, or they can be held in place by a bead or a french knot, stitched over the hole. To attach a line of sequins, secure each with a back stitch, positioning the next sequin to cover the stitch. When stitching rows side by side, the sequins of the second row should overlap the first up to the holes, to give a solid effect.

Attaching jewels and stones

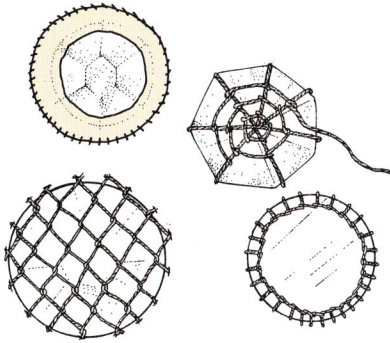

Shisha glass

2 One way of attaching a jewel or stone is to cut a ring of leather, suede, felt, or painted, non-woven interfacing, place this around the stone, covering the edges, and stitch it down to hold the stone in place.

Alternatively, the stone can be stitched in place with a spider's web or woven wheel.

If it is in keeping with the design, a stone – or another decorative object – can be held in place with a piece of net or mesh, cut to size and stitched in place round the edges.

Another commonly used method is to work buttonhole stitch around the edge, as shown.

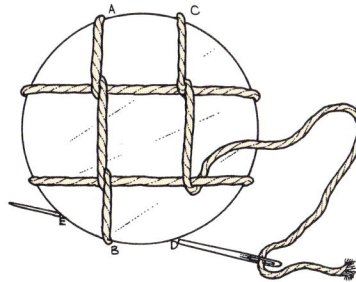

3 To attach a piece of shisha glass, hold it firmly in place and make two parallel stitches across the glass. Bring the needle out at A; pass it over and back under the first thread and then repeat the movement, taking it over and under the second thread. Insert the needle at B; bring it out at C, and work over and under again, finishing at D.

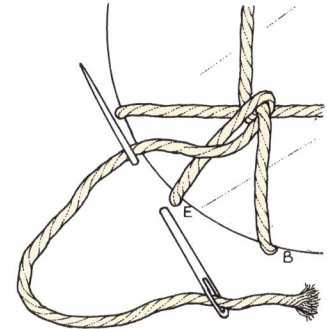

4 Bring the needle out at E and take it over the intersecting threads, as shown.

Make a small stitch close to the edge of the glass, keeping the thread below the needle.

Repeat, taking the thread over the central framework and gradually working in a clockwise direction around the edge of the glass.

Pieces of shisha glass are incorporated with reverse appliqué in this experimental piece by Judy Hope.

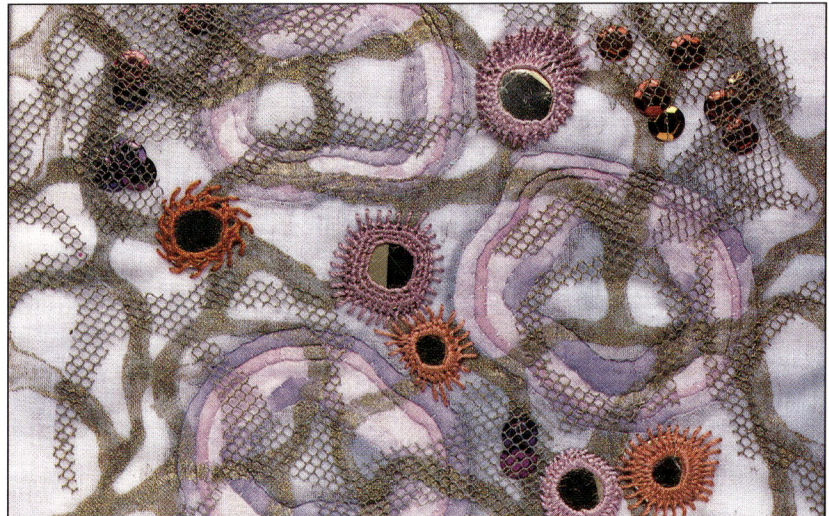

CHAPTER FIVE

USING APPLIQUÉ

Appliqué pictures, panels and wallhangings

Textiles of all types are becoming increasingly popular for wall decoration, not only in the home but also in offices, conference centres and hotels. Appliqué is a particularly versatile medium that enables imaginative craftspeople to express themselves through the creation of pictures, panels and wallhangings, using the wide variety of fabrics and materials available today.

Designs may be realistic or abstract, depending on the circumstances. If you are designing for a specific space, you should consider not only the colouring of the surrounding area, but also the proportions and scale of the room. Small pictures and panels present few problems in terms of scale, as they will fit into most settings, and the colours and textures can either tone or contrast with the rest of the design scheme; large-scale works require the bold treatment that larger areas of colour, pattern or texture can immediately bring.

When selecting fabrics for panels and pictures, there are few barriers, apart from those imposed by the actual appliqué technique, as the majority of items will require little or no cleaning. However, in view of the time and effort spent in designing and completing a piece, it is worth choosing good quality, durable fabrics.

All appliqué techniques are suitable for this form of decoration; turned-edge methods, including Hawaiian appliqué, lend themselves to striking wall-hangings, while the raw-edge techniques, such as Persian appliqué and that employing fusible web, can be used extensively, as this type of project does not need to stand up to hard wear. Reverse appliqué and inlay, with their smooth effects, would make unusual panels, and the padded methods give the opportunity for pieces of work in high or low relief. Even shadow appliqué with transparent fabrics could be incorporated in a wallhanging, to create delicate, soft imagery. Finally, many of the machine methods are of particular interest for large-scale wallhangings.

A study of hydrangeas by Sheila Cahn uses painted silk fabrics, bonded together to form the flower heads.

Presentation of work

The presentation of a work is a very important aspect of the design. Ideally, the mounting, finishing or framing should be considered at the outset as part of the whole concept – a simple appliqué can be enhanced by being beautifully mounted, whereas unsympathetic or poor framing can ruin an otherwise successful piece of work.

A professional framer will be able to advise on framing, or there are a number of ready-made frames in standard sizes which may, in some cases, be suitable. Whether a fabric picture is glazed or not is partly a matter of personal preference; glass obviously keeps it clean, but tends to reduce the tactile quality of the work. Panels with padded and three-dimensional areas are best left unglazed, in order that the texture can be fully appreciated; or they may be framed in a deep box frame, so that the work is not crushed by the glass. Non-reflective glass should be avoided, as it has a deadening effect on textiles. Even if the work is not glazed, it will require little or no cleaning – an occasional gentle brushing with a baby's hairbrush will remove dust. To clean large-scale wallhangings, cover the curtain cleaning nozzle of a vacuum cleaner with gauze and hold it a few centimetres away from the surface of the hanging. If necessary, the finished work can be sprayed with one of the stain-repellants now sold for protecting soft furnishings. Commissions for public places must usually be fire-proofed, a process that should be carried out professionally.

Preparing appliqué for framing (1, 2, 3, 4)
An appliqué panel that has been sewn on an embroidery frame should require little or no pressing. If any parts of the design have become slightly creased, press very lightly with a steam iron or with a dry iron over a damp cloth.

The finished piece is then ready to be laced over a piece of hardboard, matboard or cardboard so that it can be set in a frame. Some panels benefit from being slightly padded in order to give the appliqué a smoother appearance. This can easily be achieved, if necessary, by padding the board before lacing the appliqué over it, as shown.

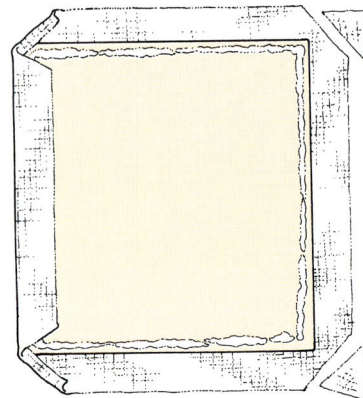

1 Measure the finished panel, excluding seam allowances, and cut a piece of hardboard, matboard or cardboard to the correct size. If there is to be a mount, include the depth of the border all around.

If you have decided to pad your panel, cut a piece of batting or flannel 2.5cm (1in.) larger all around than the hardboard. Centre the board face down on the batting. Trim diagonally across at the corners, to reduce bulk. Spread fabric glue along the edges of the board and fold fabric over it.

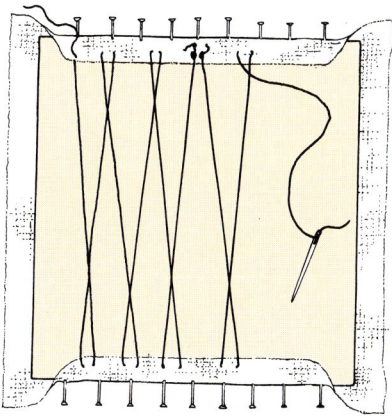

2 Prepare the appliqué by pressing, if necessary. Trim the edges, leaving them approximately 2.5cm (1in.) larger all around than the hardboard. Centre the board face down on the wrong side of the appliqué. Fold the top and bottom edges over to the back of the board and hold them in place with pins or clothes pegs.

Using strong linen thread, quilting thread or crochet cotton, and starting at the centre top and bottom, lace the two edges together with herringbone stitch, pulling the thread taut and working out to one side. Fasten securely, then return to the centre and work out to the other side.

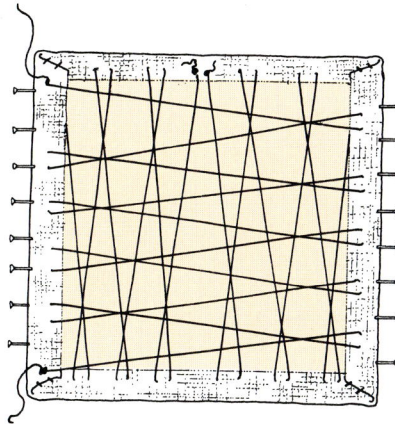

3 Check that the appliqué is positioned correctly and adjust it if necessary.

Fold the side edges to the back of the board and hold them in place with pins. Trim diagonally across at the corners to reduce bulk and make a mitred fold at each corner.

Lace the edges together, working out from the centre as before. Firmly stitch the mitre folds at the corners.

4 To neaten the work at the back, cut a piece of fabric, slightly larger than the finished appliqué. Turn the edges under so that the backing fabric is just 3mm (1/8in.) smaller all around than the mount. Pin and slipstitch the backing in place.

Mounting (1, 2)

An appliqué panel can be framed with or without a mat or border mount, depending on the individual subject and the style of the work. In many cases, however, a mat or border sets off a picture to advantage. Mat (mounting board) is available in a wide range of colours and can be cut to size with a craft knife. In addition, decorative cardboard mats (mounts) can be made in various simple geometric shapes; more intricate designs, such as window frames or arches, may reflect the elements contained in the appliqué picture.

A development of this idea is to cover the mat (mount) with fabric, using materials that contrast or tone with those used in the main design. In some appliqué pictures, three-dimensional elements, such as leaves, can actually extend beyond the perimeter to encroach on the mat (mount).

When the mount has been prepared, as shown, it can either be glued or stitched in place over the appliqué panel or, if the appliqué is being framed, the mat (mount) should first be inserted into the frame so that the appliqué can then be fitted in behind it.

Lining wallhangings (3, 4)

Wallhangings are treated differently from pictures and panels, as they are not stretched, but are allowed to hang free. They usually benefit from some type of interlining to give extra body, plus a lining to neaten the back of the work.

If you are using an interlining, which will help to give the applique a little bulk and firmness, the fabric should be selected in relation to the scale and weight of the hanging. Large-scale works require heavy-weight woven fabrics, such as tailors' canvas or sailcloth, while a non-woven interfacing will suffice for smaller pieces.

For the lining, choose a curtain lining or a similar fabric, and cut it on the straight grain, making it slightly larger than the finished appliqué. The edges are then turned under and basted, and the lining is slipstitched to the back of the work, either after a channel heading or tabs have been added, or before you attach a Velcro hanging strip, as shown overleaf.

Mounting

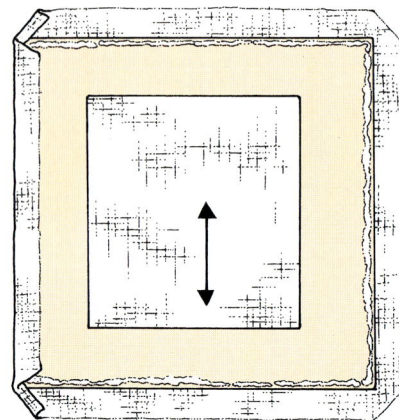

1 To prepare a fabric-covered mat (mount), cut fabric to the size of the cardboard, adding 2cm (¾in.) extra all around. (Do not cut out the centre yet.)

Centre the mat (mounting) board on the wrong side of the fabric. Trim the corners diagonally to reduce bulk, then spread fabric glue along the allowance at each side edge. Take the allowances to the back and press them firmly in place. Repeat the process, gluing the top and bottom edges to the back of the board.

Lining wallhangings

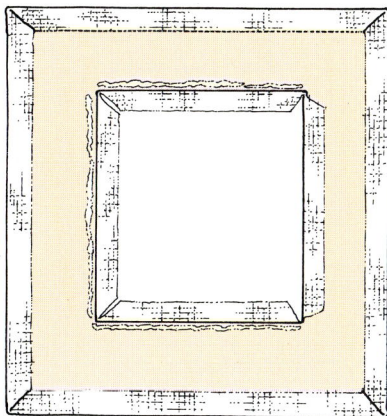

2 Cut out the central window from the fabric, cutting 2cm (¾in.) in from the cardboard edges all around. Carefully make a diagonal cut at each corner, cutting the fabric up to the cardboard corner. Apply fabric glue to the back of each allowance, as before, and fold back the fabric to complete the window.

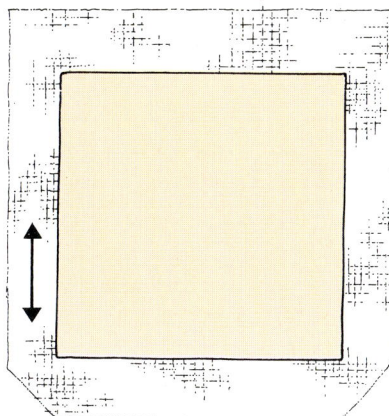

3 To interline a wallhanging, first cut a piece of interlining to the size of the finished hanging, less seam allowances, and centre it in place over the back of the work. Cutting diagonally, trim the seam allowances at the lower edges of the hanging.

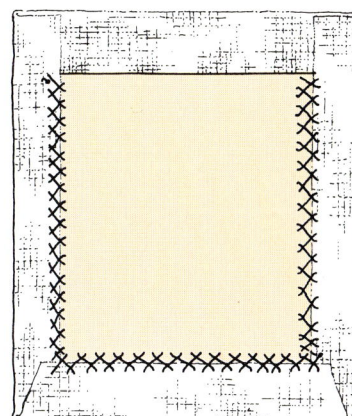

4 Fold the two sides of the hanging over the interlining and stitch them in place with herringbone stitch. Complete the lower hem in the same way. To ensure that the finished work will hang straight, curtain weights may be sewn at intervals inside the lower hem. The treatment of the top edge depends on the method of hanging.

On large-scale works, it may be necessary to lockstitch the interlining, and perhaps the lining also, to the appliqué, in order to prevent the different parts from hanging away from each other. In this case, lay the appliqué face down, with the interlining over it; fold the interlining back down the centre of the work, and lockstitch from top to bottom. Repeat, making vertical lines of lockstitch, spaced approximately 30cm (12in.) apart, and working out first to one side and then the other. Take care that the stitches do not show on the front of the work. The lining can be lockstitched in the same way, with stitches passing through lining and interlining only. Take care to leave the top edge free for your chosen hanging method.

Hanging methods

There are several ways in which to hang a finished wallhanging: a channel (1) may be stitched along the top; tabs (2, 3) can be made, forming a crenelated effect and ready to take a brass rod or a wooden pole, or you can use a Velcro strip (4). Stitch one side of the Velcro to the back of the hanging; attach the matching piece to a wooden batten and either suspend or fix this to the wall.

1 If you require a channel heading, allow for a seam allowance at the top edge, plus twice the depth of the finished channel. After turning in the side and bottom edges, turn under the top edge; bring it to the back, and machine stitch close to the folded edge, forming the channel. Alternatively, trim the top edge to leave the normal allowance, and make a separate channel, cutting a strip twice the depth of the finished work, plus two seam allowances. Turn in the short ends then, with right sides facing, machine stitch the strip to the top edge of the appliqué. Turn under the remaining long edge of the channel and stitch it in place by hand.

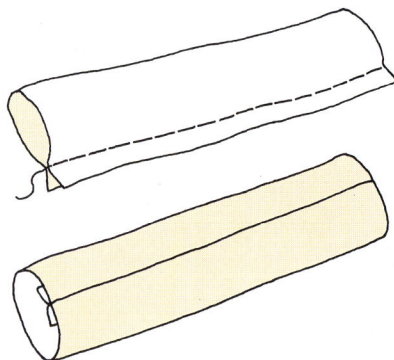

2 If you are using tabs, the size and number required will vary according to the scale of the work, but there must be a sufficient number for the work to hang smoothly. For each tab, cut a strip double the width of the tab, plus 2.5cm (1in.). Fold it in half lengthwise, with right sides together, and stitch 12mm (¼in.) from the raw edge. Turn the tube through to the right side and press, with the seam running down the centre back.

3 Fold the tab in half crosswise and attach it, with raw edges matching, to the top of the appliqué. When all the tabs are in place, bring them up, turning the top edge of the appliqué to the back in the process. Cover all raw edges by slipstitching the lining in place at the back.

Made with shot silk fabrics, this ivy hanging has appliqué shapes with frayed edges and free-standing padded leaves.

4 To attach a Velcro heading, cut a strip just short of the width of the appliqué. Separate the two sections and glue or staple the stiffer one to a wooden batten, previously attached to the wall. Machine the other Velcro strip to the back of the already lined appliqué, placing it approximately 12mm (¼in.) down from the top edge. If you do not want the stitching to show, attach the strip by hand, using herringbone stitches and making sure that, while some of the stitches catch the appliqué, and all pass through the interlining, they are not visible at the front of the work.

Boxes, bookcovers and greetings cards

Many people prefer making articles which are useful as well as decorative. Into this category fall items such as boxes, containers and bookcovers, which are interesting projects in themselves, and ideal to give as birthday or anniversary presents, as the appliqué designs can be personalized to create very special gifts.

As with all forms of functional design, consideration needs to be given to the practicalities of the article to be made. Suitable fabrics, of the correct weight and quality, should be chosen, with reference to the scale and use of the item, as well as to the particular appliqué technique. The whole design should be thought out so that the motifs figure prominently when the article is in use.

Boxes

There are several excellent books on the subject, although it is a skill beyond the scope of this book. In general, it is simpler to make a box from scratch rather than to cover an existing one. The advantages are that specific sizes and unusual shapes can be created; lids can be made to fit properly, and appliqué designs and techniques used to their full effect. The majority of boxes of this type are made from fabric-covered cardboard, with toning or contrasting quilted linings. Lids can be fitted, set in or hinged, and the inside of the box designed to suit the contents.

Bookcovers

Bookcovers are unusual items, with plenty of potential for decoration. For example, designs can reflect the contents or can be made as personalized gifts to commemorate special occasions. If you lack bookbinding expertise, there are two simple but very effective types that require no specialist skill but can easily be used as a vehicle for appliqué ideas. One of these is the slip-on cover, which can be replaced, washed, cleaned and even, sometimes, altered to fit different types of book. This type offers plenty of inspiration for designs created to reflect the book inside – the cover of a cookery book might feature food motifs; a gardening book cover might be decorated with flowers or vegetables; a scrapbook might be covered with crazy

Right Greetings cards can quickly be made for a special occasion. These three were designed by Margaret Horton.

Below Appliqué is an ideal medium for decorating small items like these boxes: a rectangular container for playing cards, designed by Margaret Horton, features an initial in silver kid and purple suede, and the pyramid-shaped pansy box, covered in shaded, dyed cotton, has free-standing flowers, decorated with machine embroidery.

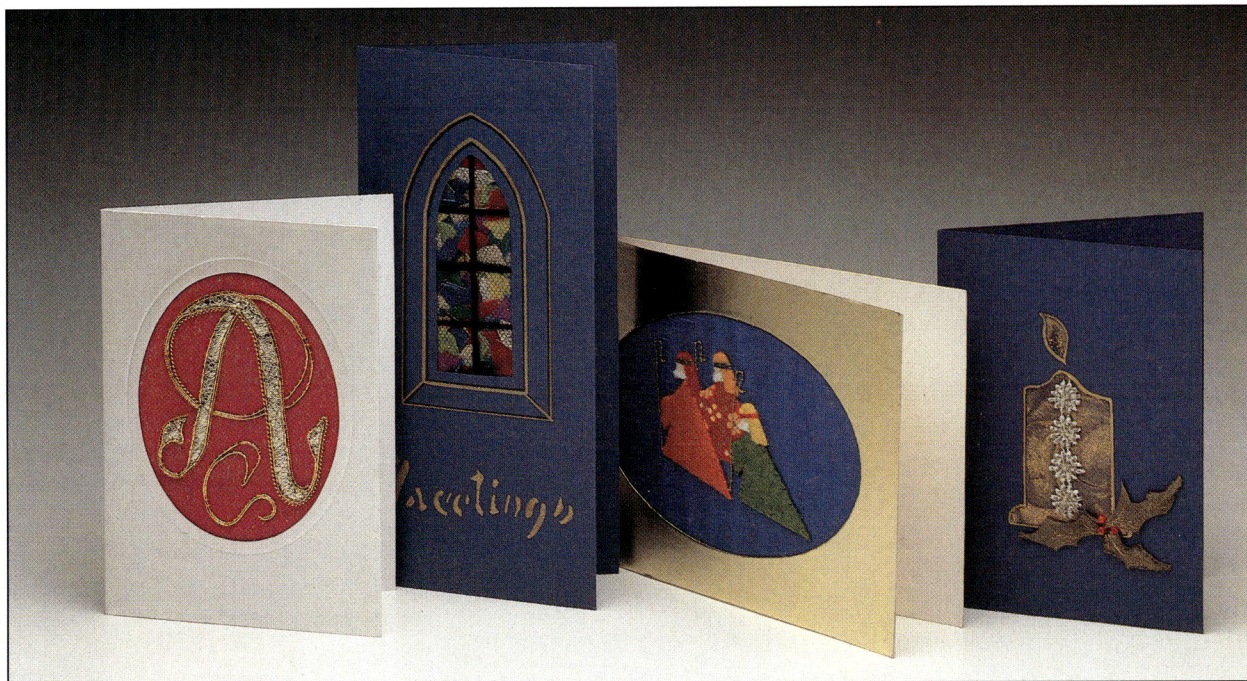

patchwork appliqué or a prayer book with religious motifs, making it an ideal gift for a wedding, christening or confirmation.

Looseleaf folders consist of two layers of fabric-covered cardboard, tied together with a leather cord or lace. These are suitable for photo albums, and might be decorated with symbols or motifs commemorating a holiday or a family celebration.

Greetings cards

Individually designed greetings cards, with windows of different shapes to house appliqué motifs or pictures, can be purchased from craft shops or by mail order. The appliqué for these miniature designs should be of fine fabric and not heavily padded – machine techniques are quick to work and lie flat, while other techniques, such as shadow and reverse appliqué, would also be suitable. The appliqué should be stretched and taped to the inner fold of the card.

Fashion appliqué

Many high fashion items are decorated with appliqué, and it is rewarding to use your skills to transform plain items into clothes that will rival or even surpass those available in the shops. If you imagine that fashion appliqué has an ethnic, 1960s feel; look about you. A casual stroll around the more exclusive boutiques will yield a host of examples of designer appliqué: delicate shadow work on silk night-wear; subtle mixtures of suede and leatherwork on belts, shoes, and bags; elegant geometric motifs in monotone contrasts of texture on sweaters, jackets, or even coats.

There are a number of ways of turning these ideas into reality, but the simplest is to add motifs or a more elaborate design to an existing garment. Applied designs may range from a slogan on a T-shirt or a satin flower added to a purchased sweater, to a ribbon border to enhance a plain blouse. The only disadvantage is that it is not always easy to add a design to a ready-made garment: you may have difficulties if it is lined, and it may not be feasible to use certain methods, such as machine appliqué, on an area that cannot be held flat for working. If you are a competent dressmaker, however, you can avoid these problems by adding your designs to simple patterns.

In either case, consideration must be given from the outset as to the fabrics, design and technique. Fabrics for appliqué should in general contain similar fibres to those of the background fabric, particularly if the garment will need to be washed frequently. Luxury garments for special occasions may incorporate unusual or dissimilar fabrics, however, giving a contrast in texture or pattern: leather or suede, for instance, can be used successfully in combination with tweed or corduroy; satin can decorate wool, or silk organza be coordinated with crepe-de-chine.

The positioning of the appliqué is one of the first considerations. Many people, particularly inexperienced designers, decide on sym-metrical designs, on the assumption that these are easier to work. In many ways, this is not the case, as the appliqué must be perfectly aligned and meticulously worked for a satisfactory result. Asym-metric arrangements, on the other hand, are less demanding in this respect and can be more interesting and flowing.

A skirt and top by Roma Mason are made in a cream silk fabric, with a design in silk and sheer organza, embellished with machine stitching.

Children's clothes

Children's clothes offer enormous scope for appliqué decoration, which is simple and quick to add and, if one of the machine methods is chosen, will stand up to frequent laundering and hard wear. An exception to the quick-and-easy rule are heirloom items, such as christening robes, where few practical considerations are necessary. Traditional floral patterns evolved from Ayrshire whitework designs can be worked in shadow appliqué or Carrickmacross lace decoration, producing a beautiful and finely worked design for a robe worthy of being handed down from generation to generation.

Accessories

Accessories are interesting to make and many do not require complicated dressmaking skills; indeed some, such as scarves and stoles, require virtually no making up, particularly if the edges can be frayed to form a fringe. In planning the design on a scarf, careful thought should be given as to the ideal placement of the appliqué, and this will depend on how the article will be worn: for a long flowing scarf, the interest should be distributed differently from that on one worn asymmetrically across the shoulder.

Gloves and a matching bag by Rosemary Watts are made in a combination of suede and leather and decorated with a punched design.

An evening belt in reverse appliqué, stitched by machine, uses metallic fabric, organza and silk. The edges of the three-dimensional leaves are finished with machine zigzag.

An old hat can easily be renovated for a special occasion with the careful application of a suitable decoration, such as an arrangement of motifs cut from scraps of fabric left over from the garment with which the hat is to be worn. Another idea is to combine two berets, using the inlay technique to cut out similar shapes from each one and relocate them in the other.

Bags come in all shapes and sizes. The simplest for the non-professional leather worker are pochettes or clutchbags and those unstructured styles, such as duffel bags and holdalls for knitting and shopping. The positioning of the design depends on the shape. Many handbags have a flap, this being an ideal area to choose, as the appliqué will be prominent when the bag is being carried or when it is set down. For other shapes, the appliqué could be centrally placed or used as a decorative border. It is simply a matter of personal choice as to the type of design chosen for application on a bag.

Belts, if they are made in contrast fabric and with interesting decoration, can transform a plain garment. Shapes cut from suede or felt can enhance a purchased soft leather belt; buckles and fastenings lend themselves to appliqué treatment, perhaps with applied motifs or with beads and jewels for evening wear, or with studs and eyelets for a more casual effect.

Soft furnishings

Whether you live in a small city apartment, a country cottage or a luxury mansion, the interior design of your home, with its accompanying soft furnishings, is an interesting project, in which the art of appliqué can play a part. Ideas can be taken from the immediate surroundings: although modern houses may have very little architectural decoration, older homes often have original features such as carvings, tiles or stained glass, from which patterns and designs can be adapted. Look, too, at the existing features, such as wallpapers and carpets – it may be possible to evolve ideas from their pattern, colour or texture. Designs can be abstract, geometric or realistic, and when you are preparing a design for a practical object, position the appliqué in relation to the end use as well as to the overall space and the shape of the item.

The same basic colour principles apply for appliqué designs for home furnishings as for pictures and panels. Consideration in this instance should also be given to the aspect of the room that you are decorating, so that in addition to reflecting your personal taste, the colours you choose will enhance the setting. For example, reds, oranges and yellows will help to add warmth to rooms that are generally dark, while fresh greens and blues would suit those that receive strong sunlight. A colour is influenced by adjoining colours and also by the intensity and quality of light to which it is subjected. For this reason, it is a good idea to make your decisions on colour in conjunction with swatches of all the furnishings in the room, placing them together in day and artificial light, and looking at them both close up and at a distance. Remember that monochromatic schemes, although safe and restful, can often benefit from an injection of a complementary colour to add a little sparkle and interest.

Many manufacturers produce coordinating plain and patterned wallpapers and fabrics, giving suggestions as to paint-work, carpets, and accessories. Although this may make interior decorating a simpler task for the inexperienced, there is a danger that any creativity on the part of the individual may be overlooked. Nevertheless, it is worth studying the schemes put together by professional designers and looking at trends in fashion.

Elspeth Kemp has used a combination of reverse and turned-edge appliqué, decorated with hand stitching, for this colourful and luxurious quilt.

Living and dining room

Soft furnishings such as cushions are the most usual items to which appliqué decoration can be added to bring interest to the living room. In a dining room, matching sets of table linen can add a touch of luxury or individuality, enhancing beautiful china and hand-thrown pottery alike. Designs can include motifs taken from your crockery, glassware or cutlery. They can repeat the patterns of the carpet or maybe a carving on a piece of furniture.

The kitchen

This often plays a central role in family life and needs a regular facelift. Changing the curtains or blinds and adding appliquéd accessories, such as oven gloves or a cover for a mixer, is often an economical way of giving a kitchen a new look. Fabrics must generally be strong and washable, and the design must also be one that will stand up to hard wear, for which reason machine appliqué is a sensible choice.

A geometric or abstract appliqué can soften the effect of a modern, streamlined kitchen, while complementing the smooth texture of ceramics, plastics and metal. Tiles and flooring can often provide inspiration for a coordinating design.

Bedrooms

The effect and mood of a bedroom scheme greatly depends on the fabrics: satins with padded appliqué for a film-star pastiche, or a restricted colour scheme, using cotton and polycotton fabrics, for an interesting but restrained effect.

Persian appliqué provides an opportunity to link toning fabrics more closely by cutting out motifs from a patterned fabric and applying them to a plain, coordinating one, either in a border or an allover arrangement. Padded appliqué is useful for headboards or chair covers, while shadow appliqué and Carrickmacross work is ideal for dressing table mats or a delicate window blind.

Items that may benefit from an applied design abound – cloths for bedside tables, quilts, scatter cushions, curtains, tissue-box covers, fabric-covered photo frames or bedlinen. You might even make an appliqué screen to divide one part of the room from another.

Above and right *Incorporating a wide variety of appliqué techniques, Aviary screen is designed to be viewed either as a whole or as four individual panels. It is made with a combination of silk fabric and suede.*

The bathroom

At first glance, the bathroom may not appear to offer much opportunity for appliquéd decoration, but the tiling or wallpaper may inspire a coordinating design for towels or even curtains or blinds. Take care, when decorating a blind, to distribute motifs evenly along the lower edge, or the blind may roll up lop-sidedly.

Shells, fish and other maritime subjects are frequently used as motifs, but it is worth searching for more unusual ideas and considering modern materials, such as plastics.

Children's rooms

Here you can allow your imagination to have full rein. A traditional nursery might feature a baby basket decorated with shadow appliqué, but a more modern treatment, using primary colours and hard-wearing machine appliqué, might have more long-term usefulness and babies enjoy bright – even garish – colours.

Look for up-to-date sources of inspiration: record sleeves will suggest design ideas for teenagers and for younger children. Floor cushions in strong fabrics and with bold designs applied to them make a popular form of seating for teenagers. Ticking can make an excellent contribution to a black and white scheme, with stripes running at different angles for a modern effect. A bedspread, cushions and curtains could all benefit from this treatment, with areas of red, yellow or bright pink for contrast.

Outdoors

Barbeques and other outdoor meals offer plenty of scope for unusual table linen or cushions. The sense of space and broader scale outdoors makes it preferable to use stronger colours and bolder designs than those that you might select for indoors.

Bright floral patterns are often used to upholster garden furniture, but a geometric appliqué, which does not compete with the beauty of nature, may make a welcome alternative. An allover trellis design, with a few well-placed leaves, might be attractive on cushions or on table linen for the garden. Items intended for outdoor use tend to be subjected to more wear and tear than indoor linen and furnishings, so washable machine appliqué is a good choice.

Pretty bedroom cushions can be produced quickly and effectively by applying ribbons on voile and adding a broderie anglaise edging.

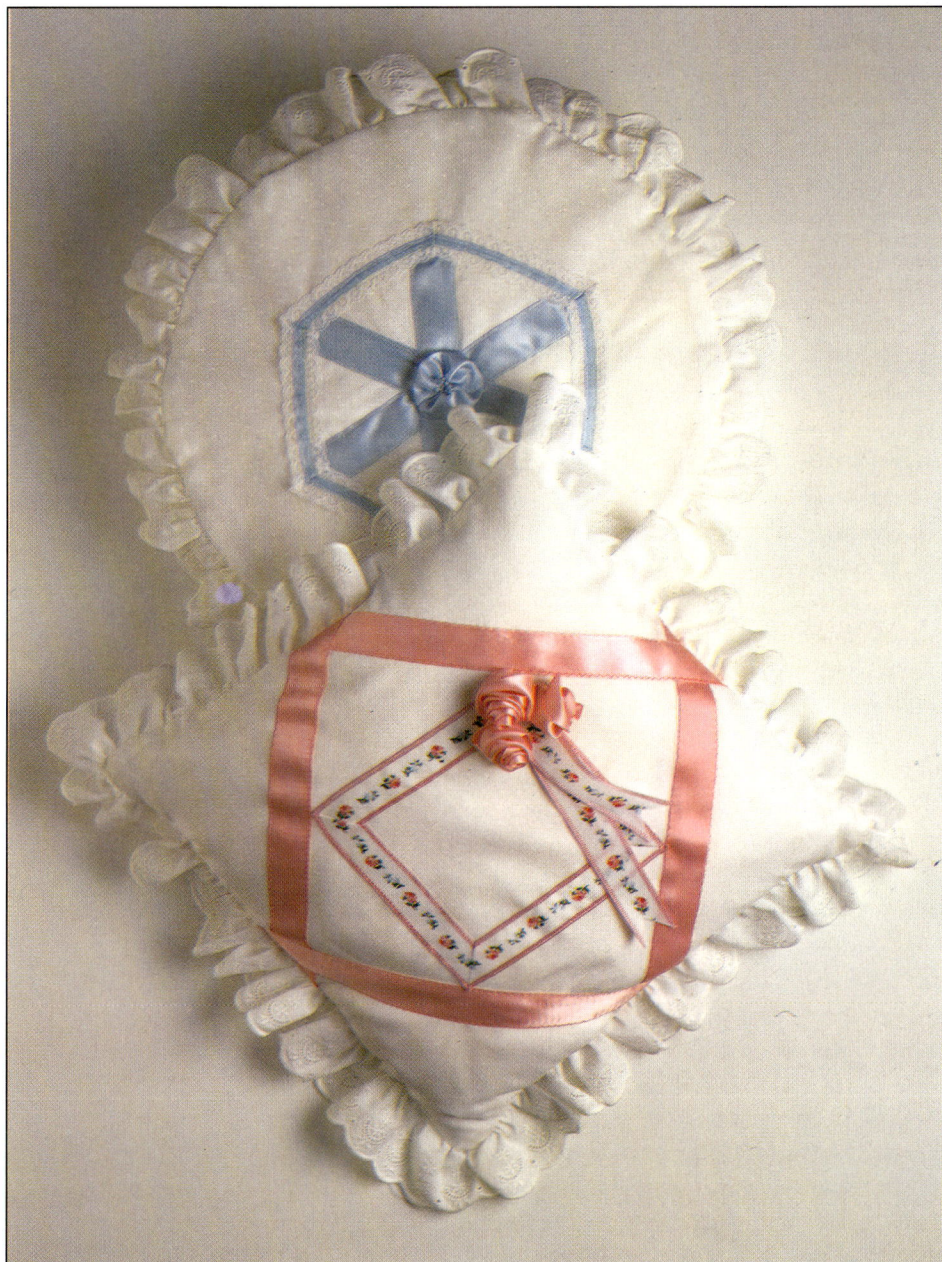

CHAPTER SIX

DESIGN

Design equipment

Design equipment for appliqué need not be expensive – you may already have in your possession some of the necessary art materials, such as a sketchbook and coloured pencils. These can be supplemented as the need arises. When buying equipment for designing, it is advisable to choose the best quality you can afford. Rather than purchasing the entire range, start with a small selection of felt tips or paints, together with three or four brushes of different sizes.

Try a few different media to decide which you enjoy using – some people prefer the freedom of working with charcoal or pastels, while others may choose pencils, crayons or felt tip pens. There are a number of paints available, including watercolour, gouache and acrylics. Each has its own particular quality – watercolour gives a transparent effect that could be suitable for delicate designs or those using sheer fabrics; gouache and acrylics are opaque and make a bolder impact.

Sketchbooks with heavy or watercolour paper are sold in different sizes and the choice depends on whether you wish to work on a small or large scale. Layout pads contain thinner paper, which can be used either for drawing or tracing; a small notebook to slip in your pocket is invaluable for making quick sketches or notes of subject matter suitable for designs.

Of particular use for appliqué design is a selection of coloured and textured papers. These can be employed for trying out ideas, as their surfaces and colours can simulate the effect of fabrics. Tissue paper is available in a range of colours which will blend if overlapped, offering an ideal way of designing for shadow appliqué and other methods that involve transparent fabrics.

Tracing paper (or greaseproof paper, which is a cheaper alternative) is an absolute essential for adapting, modifying, copying and transferring designs. It can also be used for paper patterns for

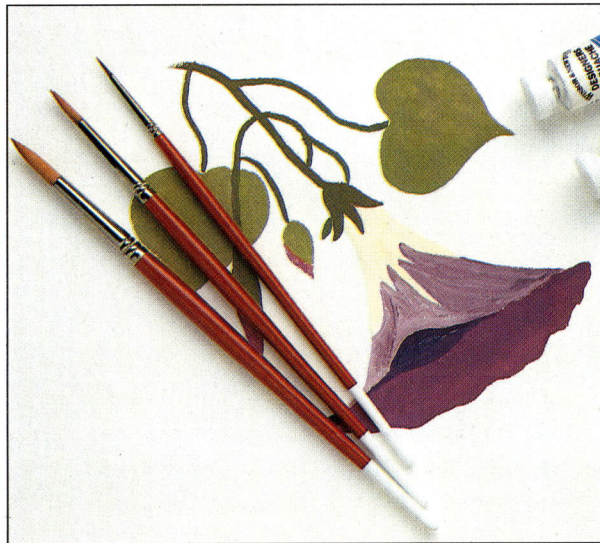

Three drawings of a morning glory flower – from left to right, in pencil, pastel and gouache – illustrate the differences between these media.

appliqué patches, but thin cardboard will be needed to make templates for repeat patterns or motifs that you wish to re-use. Dressmakers' carbon, available from fabric stores, is another useful aid for transferring designs.

A pair of scissors should be kept specially for cutting out paper. They will blunt rapidly so they will not cut fabric satisfactorily. Alternatively, use a craft knife with replaceable blades (these should be changed frequently). Used with a straight edge or metal rule and cutting board, this is essential for cutting matboard (mounts), heavy cardboard, stencils and geometric shapes.

If you are making a design from cut paper or collage, choose an all-purpose adhesive. Adhesive tape and masking tape will also be useful for holding designs in place during tracing, and double-sided tape can be helpful for collage or when making fabric or thread-bound mats (mounts). Some geometry instruments may come in handy – a compass for drawing circles and arcs, a ruler for measuring and for straight-edged designs, a protractor for measuring and dividing angles and a set- (J-)square for rectangular shapes and for mounting work. Last but not least, you will need a plastic or putty eraser so that you can alter your designs.

Inspiration for design

The creation of an original piece of appliqué must start with an idea. Your initial inspiration may come from a variety of different sources – from handling a beautiful piece of fabric, from seeing a sunset, or from the need to make an item for a particular occasion or setting. The successful fulfilment of an idea, followed through to its conclusion, will come from a series of decisions or choices. In the first instance, it is necessary to decide what you are going to make – picture, garment or useful article. Pictures and wallhangings offer few restrictions, but considerations such as durability and whether the fabrics will be washable need to be assessed for items which are worn or have a practical use, with the appropriate size, shape, fabrics and appliqué technique carefully chosen.

Inspiration usually comes from research – not necessarily an academic study, but rather from a simple and enjoyable inquiry into a subject, enhanced by a visual awareness of the world. Make a collection or scrapbook of things that attract you – magazine cuttings, postcards, shells, leaves, pebbles and so on, and look particularly at the relationship between shapes, colours and patterns. Visit museums, art galleries and exhibitions, and examine the ways in which professional artists have achieved successful designs. If you enjoy drawing, make sketches and notes of ideas or take photographs of interesting subject matter that can be adapted for appliqué design.

Design sources can be categorized into various groups. Natural forms present an unending range of subject matter – all types of plant life, such as flowers and trees; animal life, such as birds, fish and insects; and the elements of skies, rocks, water and landscape. The human form can also be a rich source of inspiration, with designs depicting people, faces, and every sort of human activity. Manmade objects range from architectural subjects, such as buildings and houses, including details such as windows and arches, to utilitarian machinery, tools, and hardware, and decorative items such as printed textiles, pottery or metalware. Any of these may become a starting point for appliqué design. Geometric forms, such as squares, circles, triangles and rectangles, can all be made into interesting arrangements.

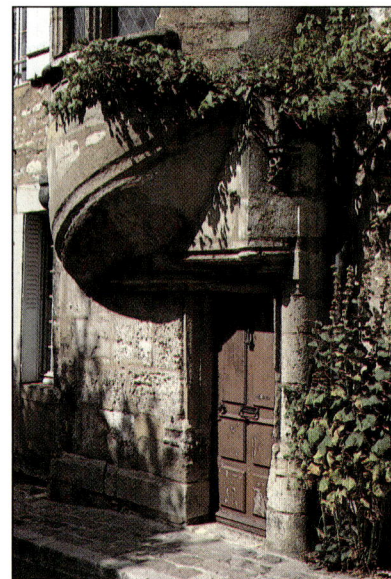

Photographs, whether of architectural features or natural objects, can be an invaluable source of design ideas, suggesting not only shapes and themes, but also attractive colour combinations.

Many designs evolve through an ability to extract from visual images the essence of an idea and to adapt and modify it for specific purposes. This can be done in a number of ways. You may prefer a totally naturalistic approach (1), using a design taken from a carefully drawn picture or from a photograph, with the basic shapes, colours and textures emulating, as far as possible, the actual image. A realistic design may, of course, be adapted so that the colours are changed or the emphasis altered, while the image still retains its overall outline. A stylized design (2) is one that has been adapted from realism, so that the inherent nature of the motif still remains, although the outline or shape may have been changed and additional decorative features included. These types of design are very suitable for appliqué, as they are usually bold in concept. An abstract design (3) may be one that has evolved from realism but has been so altered and adapted that the original is barely recognizable; another type of abstract design is pure pattern (4), based on geometric or random shapes and lines.

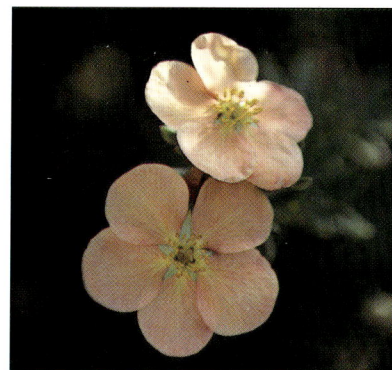

Designing for appliqué

Designing for appliqué may consist of scattering – apparently at random – a selection of individual motifs or devising a precise and ordered border pattern. Alternatively, you may wish to create a picture or panel of abstract or realistic subject matter. Traditionally, the types of design most suited to the medium are those that incorporate simple shapes – indeed one of the advantages of appliqué is that an immediate and bold effect can be rapidly achieved.

A successful work of appliqué should incorporate the basic elements of proportion and balance, an awareness of colour, pattern and texture, as well as competent execution of the basic skills. You may already have a talent for design and be able to draw well – certainly most people can sketch well enough to make a simple plan – and sometimes it is only necessary to move elements or motifs around until a satisfactory arrangement is achieved. Because appliqué is a technique that is inherently concerned with shape and mass, the shapes must be placed in such a way that they please the eye and are of a suitable scale and proportion.

Proportion, which is the comparative relationship between one area and another, is a particularly important consideration. The overall size of the work may well be dictated by its use or surroundings. For example, a picture may be destined for a particular wall, a garment must fit the wearer and a soft furnishing item must be in scale with its setting. The individual elements of an appliqué design should also relate in size to the overall area, bearing in mind that the background must be recognized as an important part of the design.

A symmetrical design is one that is perfectly balanced, each side exactly mirroring the other. Although not necessarily the most interesting type of design, it has a formality and order that makes it suitable for repeat borders on table or bed-linen, and for decoration on the front of a garment. An asymmetrical design is one that is not exactly reflected on either side. There does, however, need to be a balance – if a large motif is placed on one side, it will probably need to be supported by several smaller ones on the other. Some designs have a focal point that can be placed centrally or just off centre. This focal point should attract the eye by virtue of its size, colour or contrast of texture, and there should, in addition, be smaller points of interest, which can be carefully placed to enhance the overall balance. If the various elements in a design are linked or overlapped, the effect will be an integrated whole rather than a set of unrelated, fragmented motifs.

Harmonious designs are those that include shapes, colours and textures of a similar nature. By adding a small amount of contrast to this harmony, an appliqué arrangement of shapes can be enlivened and be made more interesting, while a carefully arranged pattern of motifs of a similar shape or colour will give interest to soft furnishing items or to clothes.

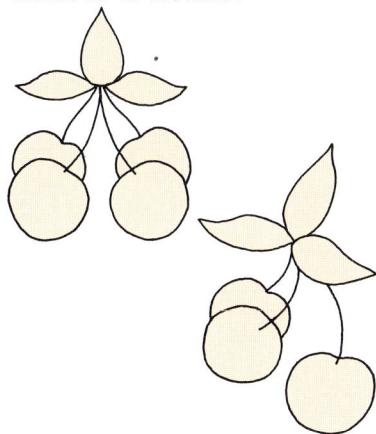

1 An asymmetrical motif generally looks more natural and also more interesting than a formal, strictly symmetrical one. There does, however, need to be a sense of balance, just as there would in an overall design.

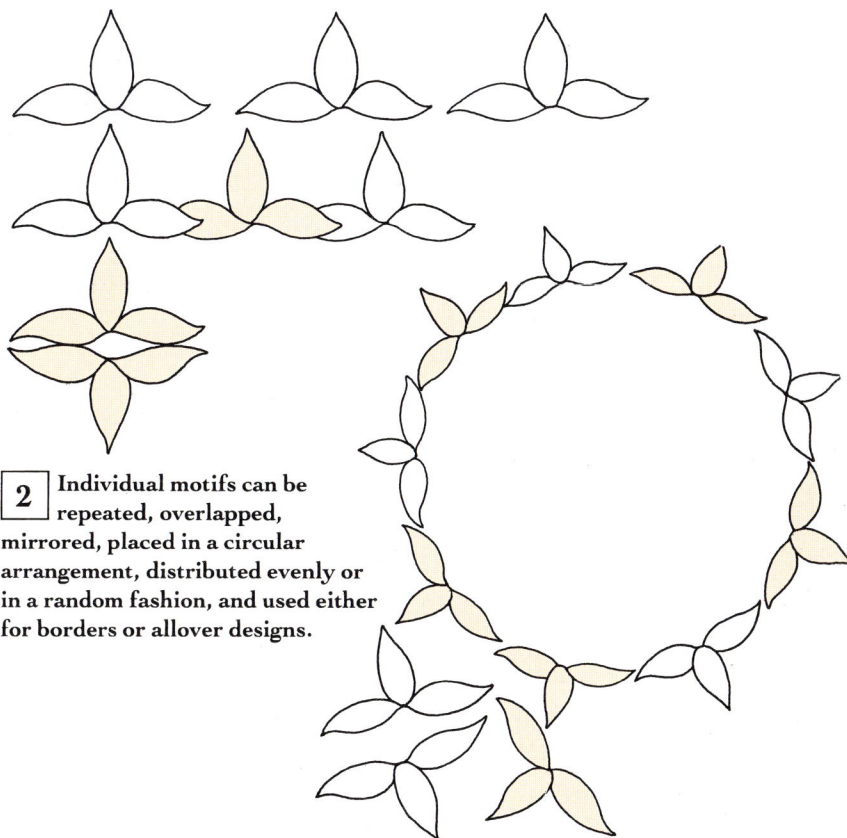

2 Individual motifs can be repeated, overlapped, mirrored, placed in a circular arrangement, distributed evenly or in a random fashion, and used either for borders or allover designs.

Colour

The creation of colourful designs is one of the attractions of appliqué, which is one of the quickest methods of applying large expanses of colour to a textile design. For this reason, appliqué is frequently chosen by theatrical designers, who use this technique to make instant impact, especially from a distance.

A good sense of colour can be an intuitive talent – we all express our personality in the colours we choose to decorate our homes and for the clothes we wear. Most people have favourite colours and those they hate – indeed colours have characteristics that most will agree upon. Reds are bold and friendly, while browns are homely and restful. Yellows provide cheerfulness and sunshine; greens may be crisp and fresh, and blues are calm and serene.

The choice of colour may well be the starting point for a design – you may wish to make cushions to match wallpaper and carpets in a room, or create table linen that harmonizes with your chinaware. In this case, look closely at the colours that the professional textile designers and potters have used – there may well be unexpected combinations of hues that could lead you to interesting colour schemes.

Some knowledge of the basic principles of colour and tone will enable you to develop your own colour ideas and to produce tonally balanced works of appliqué. A colour wheel is a device that shows the colours of the rainbow arranged in a circle. On one side are the warm reds and yellows, and on the other are the cool greens and blues. Placed equidistant on the wheel are the primary colours – the pure hues of red, yellow and blue from which, with black and white, all other colours come. Between these are the secondary colours, which are achieved by mixing equal quantities of the two adjacent primaries together. Thus red and yellow make orange, blue and red make purple, and yellow and blue make green.

The importance of tone in appliqué cannot be over-emphasized. This is the intensity of colour – whether it is light or dark. A tint is made by adding white to a primary or secondary colour; a shade is made by adding black. Dark tones, which absorb light, usually recede, while lighter ones advance. In the same way, warm vibrant colours, such as red and bright orange, can be placed in the

In this colour wheel, formed with ruched fabrics, the tints are in the centre, gradually radiating through hues to shades on the outside.

foreground or used as a focal point, while muted or cool colours, such as pale blue, can achieve an effect of depth or distance in a design.

A harmonious colour scheme is one that uses the colours that appear next to one another on the colour wheel. They will blend together well and create an undemanding and restful design. Contrasting colours, also known as complementary colours, are those that are on opposite sides of the wheel. Thus, red is complementary to green, yellow to purple, and blue to orange. Black and white, of course, are also contrasting colours. Designs formed from contrasting colours will be more vibrant and exciting than harmonious schemes, while including a small amount of contrast can enliven an otherwise uninteresting piece of work.

Pattern

Appliqué was traditionally worked with plain fabrics, but the use of patterned materials can inspire ideas, bringing interest and individuality to a piece of work.

Whether they are printed, woven or knitted, patterned fabrics should be chosen with care for inclusion in a piece of work. It is essential to select patterned fabrics by viewing them, not only close up but also at a distance, in order to determine the relative tonal values. In particular, the scale of the pattern should be examined in relation to the size of the appliqué patches and to the design as a whole. Small-scale patterns and those of a medium size, especially if they contain just two shades of one colour, create background interest for large-scale areas, without adding too much emphasis. Those with more strongly contrasting tones should be used for patches that are of greater importance in a design.

Large-scale florals or chintzes, and the Paisley designs that appear on furnishing fabrics, are usually multi-coloured. It is worth studying the scale and tonal values carefully before you include patterns of this type: if used in large pieces, they may be very dominant. It is often possible, however, to cut out and use small pieces of a large-scale pattern.

For appliqué panels and pictures, using the back of the fabric in contrast or preference to the front is a possibility that should not be overlooked. On printed fabrics the reverse is usually paler in tone than the right side, and this fact could well be used for an appliqué landscape where this can soften the tone of the background area. On some woven fabrics, such as brocade, the design is completely reversed, so that those areas that are shiny on one side appear dull on the other, and vice versa. This characteristic can be used with interesting results.

A crazy patchwork by Prue Dobinson incorporates hand-painted and dyed silk fabrics with feather stitch outlines.

Texture

Most appliqué techniques are concerned with the addition of fabrics, which in themselves create texture on the background material. Padded methods produce high or low relief, while freestanding or three-dimensional motifs may create bold sculptural effects. The application of beading or embroidery stitches may add to the range of textures, and fabrics can be manipulated in different ways for attractive surface decoration. In reverse appliqué, the areas of interest are defined by the lower levels of underlying fabrics.

Texture, of course, appears in everything around us. Start to become aware of the textural effects that occur both in nature and in manmade objects. Look at the roughness of the gravel path, the ridges of tree bark or the smoothness of leaves. Indoors, the tactile qualities of a wallpaper, a carpet or a piece of furniture may draw your attention for the first time.

The actual construction of some fabrics is inherently textural – they may have a slub, or a bouclé or hairy surface; they may be closely or loosely woven and some, such as velvet, towelling or fur, possess a pile. Some finishing processes – glazing, for example – produce an alternative surface texture.

The tactile quality of a fabric may well be the characteristic that initiates its choice for a piece of work, either because of its attractiveness or because the surface qualities bear a close resemblance to that of the subject – a shiny red satin for rosy apples, a rough tweed for a ploughed field or fur fabric for animal designs in a nursery.

Texture can be enhanced by contrast, that is by placing a smooth shiny area close to a dull rough fabric – tweed with cotton, velvet next to silk. A design that includes changes of textural effect will have greater interest than one that is confined to fabrics of a similar type. Texture can also create effects of light and shade in a work.

Smooth shiny fabrics reflect the light and will therefore be more prominent in a design, while dull fabrics, such as fine wool, absorb light and are more likely to recede. These characteristics can be exploited to the fullest extent in pictures and wallhangings, but for garments and soft furnishings the practicalities of washing and ironing may have to be taken into consideration.

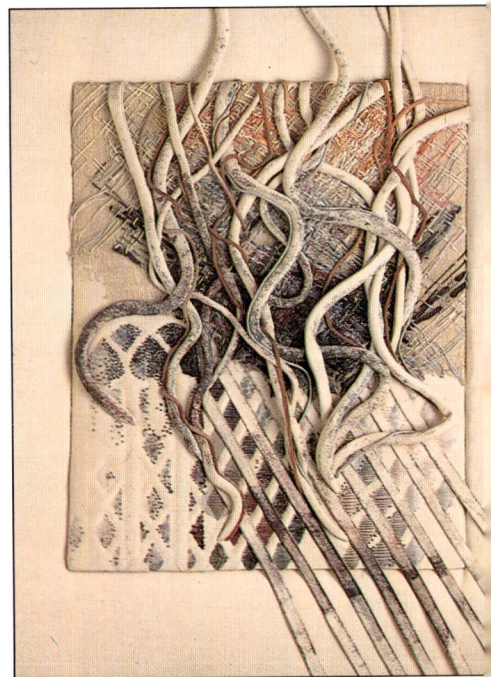

Above *This silk and scrim panel by Sheila Cahn is based on tree formations. The background is printed and stitched to form a basis for the rouleaux, which have been threaded with wire, creating a sinuous and highly textured effect.*

Right *One of the pleasures of appliqué is finding the ideal fabric, with exactly the texture that is needed to suggest an image or set up an interesting contrast.*

The texture that appliqué produces can create interest in all types of work. In particular, padded and three-dimensional appliqué can vary the surface of a design and produce exciting results. Batting (wadding) will create a squashy texture, whereas if you use felt, the effect will be finer; shapes cut from foam rubber can raise an area to high relief, and pieces of fabric-covered cardboard can give sleek and precise outlines.

Design methods

An ability to sketch or draw well is an obvious advantage when you are embarking on an appliqué design, which can be developed from any type of art work, ranging from a simple line drawing to a full-scale painting. If, however, you lack confidence when it comes to making designs, there is no reason to despair – there are many very effective ways of creating a design without first producing a freehand drawing.

Adapting drawings and photographs

Photographs can easily be adapted and simplified to make appliqué designs. The photograph can either be one of your own – your house or garden, perhaps, or holiday scene – or you might take it from a magazine or a book. In fact, the technique given here works equally as well for a drawing or painting as for a photograph.

Whatever your source of inspiration, it will probably need to be simplified to make it suitable for appliqué. Very often, only a portion of it will be needed, so isolate the most appropriate area by making a view-finder from two L-shaped pieces of paper or card and moving these around to 'frame' different parts of the picture.

To simplify a design, make a tracing of the main elements of the drawing or photograph, excluding any intricate details, while still retaining the definition and essence of the shape. Bear in mind that most appliqué techniques rely on shape rather than lines for their effectiveness; narrow areas and points may be difficult to achieve by some methods, although complicated shapes can be applied with fusible web.

Designing with paper

Many people are nervous about creating designs and feel that they are not good enough artists to sketch or draw, but they are very happy to cut out paper shapes for use in appliqué design. Any type of paper may be employed – collect together a range of different colours and textures. Some are manufactured specially for design purposes, but you will probably already have scraps of gift-wrap or wallpaper in stock. It is a help to be able to relate these to the type of fabric you

Left and right *This design by Sheila Cahn, featuring leaves and berries, began with a photograph, which was then simplified in the watercolour sketch, before being translated into appliqué shapes on a painted voile background.*

Below *Spiky paper shapes formed the initial design inspiration for this star-shaped appliqué by Sheila Cahn.*

intend to use – a corrugated paper might simulate corduroy, a smooth shiny wrapping paper could represent satin. Tissue or tracing paper can be used for shadow appliqué designs, for which transparent fabrics are required.

First experiments can be made by cutting out simple geometric or random shapes and placing them on a contrasting background. Move them around, overlapping them or arranging them in rows, circles or irregular patterns; take careful notice of the spaces between the shapes, as the background area constitutes an important part of the design. Strips of paper are helpful when you wish to plan out the colours and proportions of a ribbon appliqué.

Folded paper designs
Designs for borders and friezes, such as those made by children, can be created by cutting shapes on an accordion-pleated strip of paper.

Repeat motifs
The simplest way to work out repeats is to cut out several identical paper shapes and arrange them to form patterns. The motifs need not, of course, be the same size: changes in scale can make a repeated image appear to advance or recede, giving a feeling of movement and perspective.

Exploded designs
These have an inherent quality of harmony, as all the elements are cut from a single piece of paper, such as a square or circle. The cut shapes are then placed on a contrasting background and 'exploded' or moved apart until a satisfactory arrangement develops. This method is particularly useful for adding appliqué to a specific area, such as the yoke of a dress. Cut two pieces of paper, one the shape and size of the finished piece and the other the same shape but considerably smaller. Cut this last into several pieces, place these on the background paper and gradually draw them apart, thereby evolving a harmonious design.

Enlarging or reducing a design

If your original drawing, sketch or reference material is of a scale which needs to be altered in some way to make it appropriate for your intended design, there are several ways to tackle this. You can simply re-draw it to the required size and shape or use a photocopier to enlarge or reduce it. The third method, although it appears at first sight to be somewhat complicated, offers the added possibility of elongating or distorting a design. This is sometimes necessary if a design needs to fit into a specific space. It can also make an interesting variation on a conventionally proportioned motif.

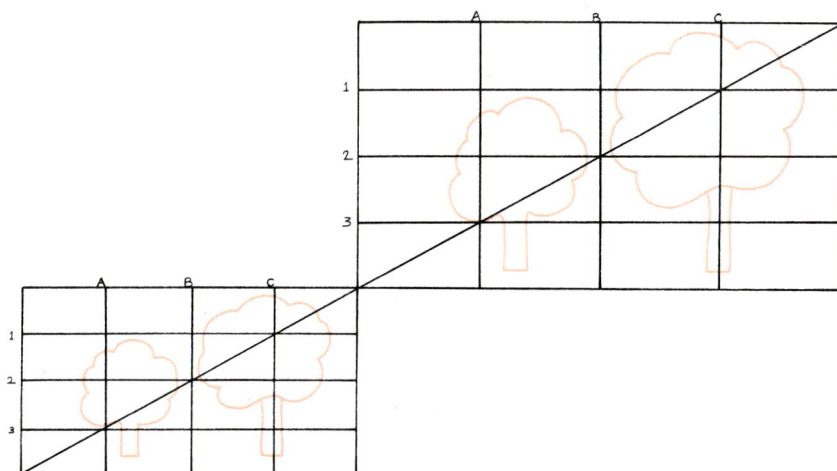

1 Make a tracing of the original drawing and enclose it within a rectangle or square. Divide this into a grid of horizontal and vertical lines by halving, quartering and further dividing, as necessary. The more complicated the design, the more grid lines will be required.

2 Draw a diagonal from the bottom left-hand corner to the top right, extending it as shown. Extend the adjoining sides of the rectangle and draw a new, larger rectangle, making sure that the top right-hand corner also lies on the diagonal. Divide this into a grid, with the same number of lines as the first grid. Identify the lines on both, using numbers for lines running one way and letters for crossing lines. Copy the design section by section. Use the same technique to reduce a drawing, simply making a smaller second rectangle instead of a larger one.

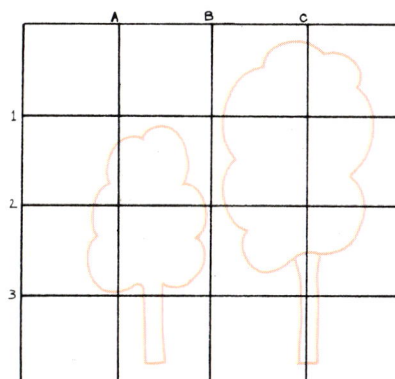

3 To elongate or distort a design, prepare the first grid as above, but omit the diagonal. Draw a rectangle to whatever dimensions you require and divide it with a grid of the same number of lines as the first grid. The small rectangles of the second grid may be narrower or wider than those of the first. Copy the design in the normal way, making minor adjustments as necessary, to allow for the distortion.

INDEX

ACKNOWLEDGMENT

I should like to thank all those friends and students, including those from Hampstead Garden Suburb Institute, the London College of Fashion and Cassio College, Watford, who kindly lent their work for inclusion in this book. I am also grateful to Messrs C. F. Offray & Son Ltd for supplying ribbons and to Madeira Threads (UK) Ltd for their embroidery threads.

NOTE: All work is by the author unless otherwise credited.